SOCIOLOGY OF CULTURE AND MUSIC

SOCIOLOGY
OF
CULTURE AND MUSIC

Dr. Ishrat Jahan

KANISHKA PUBLISHERS, DISTRIBUTORS
NEW DELHI 110002

KANISHKA PUBLISHERS, DISTRIBUTORS
4697/5-21A, Ansari Road, Daryaganj
New Delhi -110 002
Phones : 2327 0497, 2328 8285
Fax : 011-2328 8285
E-mail : kanishka_publishing@yahoo.co.in

Sociology of Culture and Music
First Published 2011

ISBN : 978-81-8457-290-2

PRINTED IN INDIA

Published by Madan Sachdeva for Kanishka Publishers, Distributors, 4697/5-21A, Ansari Road, Daryaganj, New Delhi-110 002, Typeset by Sunshine Graphics, Delhi, and Printed at Rajdhani Printers, Delhi.

Introduction

We live amid an era of cultural pluralism where mass audiences enjoy privilege of participation and the right to make judgments about works of art. Co-existence of plural cultural beliefs in the social world is one of the central reasons masses have achieved access to the field. Furthermore, the mass can afford whatever they want to purchase. Appreciation of Higher Art always involved a small audiences or viewers in pre-industrial societies. In Europe the consumers of high culture was confined to members of economic, political and religious institutions. In case of India the appreciation came from Raja, Maharaja and landed aristocracy. Over many decades we profoundly experience the dominance of the masses in the artistic process and influence of their taste in cultural products due to shift in socio-political ecology. Here I am trying to give a message that popular culture strenuously influencing the artistic field due to technical reproduction and art trade which had its root in 1900s. Popular culture provides an easy access to those individuals whose musical ability, experience in music production is quite inadequate and who can guess public demand and whose activities are directed to populist mission. Interestingly nowadays we notice that heterogeneous songs are available to select hello tune, welcome tune, caller tune, dialers tune in telecommunication. It is obvious that human's drive towards music is also mounting music production, reproduction, distribution, consumption of music at a large. To speak bluntly it is not merely popular songs but a few symphonies of populist taste also include cell phone ringtone. Today music acts as a sign and a device of mass communication. As mentioned earlier popular music or amateur music widely dominate the field of music. Because a piece of classical music being phenomena requires a minimum of understanding grammar, musical events a performer creates. Human beings at different stages of life gradually understand, perceive and conceptualize the elements of classical music. The fact is masses are deprived of such potentials.

Now a question arises what really higher music articulates?

Higher music is an expression of creativity and intellectuality wherein a master musician upholds the norms inherent in the legitimate field and community of the artiste himself.

In higher music, musical expressions are abstract or symbolic by nature. Musical expressions are abstract in the sense that the composer or musician expresses feelings and emotions in a non-concrete manner. Musical pieces are bound with musical materials i.e. construction of musical sound, imagination, interpretation of style, belief about particular piece, ideatation and motivation of the creator. It denotes and makes a difference between a piece of music and reciting poetry. In other words, music is metaphor of abstract feeling. Classical music or higher music has its base in non-concrete feelings. The technique of master musician's sound construction is related to aesthetic logic that may evoke or enhance emotions in listeners.

Personality researcher Sloboda remarked:

> ... Music is capable of arousing in us deep and significant emotions. The aesthetic delight in a sound construction, through emotions like joy and sorrow which music sometimes evokes or enhances, to the simple relief from monotony, boredom or depression which everyday musical experiences can provide (Sloboda, 1885: p. 1).

In Sloboda's remark we find that music acts as therapy. Thus making quality music is the manifestation of self-expression of culturally constructed belief system and individuality. Organization of musical materials has its own nature. Musical sound derives from regular frequency wherein noise or disturbing sound originates from irregular frequency. Musical sound comprises three distinct features, namely (*i*) *Pitch*: Tones produced in vocal organ or in instrument may not be same. It is because of pitch. For example, *ni* is higher than *dha*. Each note contains certain frequency. If someone presses the keys of a harmonium from left to right than one will experience that each succeeding note is higher than the preceding one. Pitch depends upon the number of vibrations or frequency of the note. For instance, *sa* of Indian music has frequency of 240, *ga* contains frequency of 300. Naturally *ga* has higher pitch than the *sa*. Some folk instruments for example, Ektara do not have different pitch other than only pitch *sa*.

(*ii*) *Intensity of sound production*: Intensity of notes implies to degree of force placed upon the notes. This degree of intensity causes louder or softer sound. Intensity depends on the amplitude of vibration. In case of louder sound amplitude remains greater.

(*iii*) *Quality of sound*: Human voice differs from one another due to quality of the tone produced. The quality of a musical note is determined by the existence of harmonics or overtones. The quality of instrumental playing or human voice seems different because of the different number or relative strength of the overtones or harmonics produced by each as a note is sounded.

There are seven notes both in western and Indian music system.

In Indian musical term these notes have been named *Sadaja, Rishabha, Gandhara, Madhyama, Panchama, Dhaivata, Nishada,* During singing the first letter of each note is used. Thus the performer of vocal music uses during singing *sa, re, ga, ma, pa, dha, ni.* These seven notes together constitute *Saptaka.*

The pre-requisite of making music entails creativity. Musical scholars conceive music as medium of expression. Now the quest comes what music has to do with expression.

What really music articulates, scholars of the West encounter differences by their divergent opinions.

The bottom line in music expresses feeling of creative social beings symbolically. The concept of symbolic feeling can be explained as an organization of sound implied either by vocal organ or instrumental devices wherein expression takes place by means of musical notes, concentration, sentiment, musical knowledge, imagination, ideatation of the music maker. More precisely music is a medium to express feelings in abstract manner. In case of vocal music composition of a *raga* or *bandish* may embody some literary value but feeling is basically manifested by highly abstract sound structure.

Now the quest is what listeners search from music? Listeners are not uniform in terms of attitude and knowledge. Cultivated listeners search for beauty and aesthetic delight, on the other hand mass consumption aims at entertainment because their ears are not trained to understand pure music.

Musicians as a distinct social class and occupational group significantly play a role in the production of cultural goods in relation to other agent's active participation. His/her role in contemporary, socio-economic structure (Principles of capitalism and era of media) largely reveal an opposition as higher music was consumed by the elite of the society before the emergence of capitalist mode of production when its production aimed in keeping with creation for own self, to the artiste community and for the cultivated audience to a lesser extent.

It is conspicuous to everyone that in contemporary cultural ambiance traditional music and musicians confront some unavoidable social forces i.e., the capitalist, entertainment industry, changing technology and consumer demand. All popular forms of music resulted from limited aesthetic value, far more than that popular music is harmonizing the external determinants (Market principles) or making an adjustment with objective social relations of music, in other words, demand of the public. Most public are incapable of making aesthetic differentiation of works of art i.e. inability to perceive what is pure or good or poor music.

The focus and objective of my work is not directed to accuse popular music alone for wearing commercial principles at the same time it intends to view classical music not completely innocent in its social relations and aesthetic logic.

I have adopted an empirical approach to study Indian music to assert relationship among variables of social worlds and agents of creation. I presume that any cultural activity is not isolated from other social classes and social forces. Secondly, variables have been analyzed in relation to a given period of socio-cultural context.

Defining Concepts

Middle Class: Middle class is a distinct social class in highly stratified society. The indicators of middle class are education, profession and income.

The term dilemma has been used to denote confusion and contradiction in the world of music. *Karnataka* music system does not include in the discussion in this book.

Indian Classical Music is confined to the discourse of *Hindustani* Music of North India and Bangladesh.

Gharana: In musical sense *gharana* means distinctive singing or instrumental style created by its founder and the knowledge would be imparted to kinsmen to disciples outside the *gharana* through *guru shishya* tradition at least for three generations to establish the base of *gharana.*

Achievements refer to progress both qualitative and quantitative aspects in case of Indian music.

Raga: The soul of Indian music is *Raga. Raga* has resulted from an evolutionary process. It is a melodic pattern of consistent notes (*Swaras*). Presentation of *raga* may vary from artiste to artiste on account of individual talent, knowledge, quality of training and varying expression artistes follow according to their aesthetic consideration.

Tala: Tala is another integral part of Indian music. *Tala* is a movement based on beats. *Tala* (Time) harmonizes to create order and balance in music. Tempo (*Laya*) is another feature of *Tala,* which has three expressions i.e. *Vilambita, Madhya,* and *Drut laya.* Tala is the basic component of singing, instrumentation and dancing. Tala is the result of evolutionary process. In the Vedic period there was rhythm but not *tala. Tala* came into practice in post vedic period. In this period rhythm and tempo came to be known as *laya*. Movement is the base of *laya*. *Laya* is an equal interval of pauses. *Vilambita laya* indicates slow tempo, *madhya laya* indicates medium tempo and *druta laya* indicates faster tempo. *Tala* measures *kala* or time of singing, playing of instrument.

Enormous literature on Indian music and its contents depict basically historical analysis or aesthetic logic of music. Although a few foreign writers e.g. Neuman, Hamilton has focused on sociological aspects of music but this approach among Indian scholars seems to be almost absent. Taking music beyond narrow realm of merely historical accounts in connection with theories of music, my attempt is to analyze music critically in relation to social classes and culture. I have taken a deeper interest in cultural theories of Western Marxist in my work.

As stated earlier, my objective is to focus music from theoretical perspective of Marxist intellectuals, to mention a few of them W. Benjamin, T. Adorno, P. Bourdieu, A. Gramsci whose theories inaugurate academic research in the West. Classical social thinker Max Weber and many other also include in discussion ahead.

To come to point of relevance the coming of modernity and reaction of the intellectuals, the gulf between high/pop culture, why does stagnation in musical forms happen? How do musicians contribute in the education and production system of a society? How their role has changed in the market economy? Has technology benefited higher music? Chapters ahead will search for these answers through debate.

Author

Contents

Contents

1

Modernity and Middle Class

Cultural analysis of any art, music or other forms includes several factors i.e., cultural content, social world, creator, receiver (audience or benefactor). Before modernity the guarantee of material security of any higher form of art was linked to the patronage of the elite, aristocracy of a society. To Edward W. Said, "Music, like literature, is practiced in a social and cultural setting but it is also an art whose existence is premised undeniably on individual performance, reception or production". Edward Said recognizes ambience and network of music production. Higher culture is essentially a valuable part of tradition which bears identity of a society. However the world of art counts on many factors. Of these factors, motivation of the creator and its creation, users also determine the process of change in the artistic field.

As we know *Gharanas* in *Khayaal* singing emerged as a family tradition but in the course of time failed to sustain its one of the key conditions such as transformation of knowledge within lineage as old elitist patronage started to fall apart.

During the last decades of the Mughal rule external political force was imposed on India which had a greater impact on socio-political and cultural ambience. Prior to independence initially institutionalization of traditional music in some parts of India for instance, Pune, Bombay and Calcutta and performance sponsored by institution with a view to restore traditional art music speak little similarity as artistes performed in court settings. This time audiences comprised English educated upper and mostly middle class. Both in India and Europe a particular portion of middle class encouraged higher culture despite there remain major differences between Indian and European middle class.

In the last quarter of eighteenth century Western Europe was going through social transformation. The change generated conflicting perspective among the intellectuals of the West; some were reactionary, while others were radical of the shift. Modernity in India started with the impact of colonial rule. Second phase of modernization took place after independence. On the road to westernization Indian society did not indicate similar measure like Europe.

At this particular time Western Europe received a push into traditional culture due to new technology which engendered mass media under the influence of industrial revolution. In the language of sociologists such societal transformation is called modernity.

Theorizing Modernity

Modernity in one sense has come to mean industrialization, capitalism, nation-state, science and technology, democracy, energy use, rationalization, liberalism, nationalism, new professions, and new social classes in pluralist social structure of burgeoning urban life. Marxist sociologists increasingly view modernity along with a series of social indicators such as socialism, communism etc.

In another sense, modernity is an aesthetic movement built on break from traditional form which does not represent reality (mimetic) for example, music of Schoenberg, Webern, Berg), in painting impressionist Matisse, Picasso; in literature British writers Joyce, James, Yeats, Eliot and so on. In the West modernist movement in music, art and literature was affirmed with consistency, depth, innovation and individual genius that sought for autonomy of creativity.

Modernity in Intellectuals' Ideas

For Marx, modernity was characterized by alienation, exploitation due to industrialization, domination of the capitalists in the realm of economy.

To remark about modernity in which capitalism exists Marx and Engels wrote: It has converted the physician, the lawyer, the priest, the man of science, into its paid wage-labourers (Marx and Engels, 1967: p. 82).

To Weber modernity started with rationalization process of economy, bureaucracy where economic sphere became separated from the domain of politics. Weber also defined notation system in occidental music as rational. But Weber noted that people during societal transformation were increasingly imprisoned in the iron cage of rationality.

Emile Durkheim explained modernity in terms of organic solidarity and anomie. Although organic solidarity (expansion of production by specialized division of labour) recognized some sort of freedom, individual skill, at the same time it weakened traditional norms.

Simmel's modernity reveals the nature of modern urban life where money is a transforming force in relation to exchange. In the philosophy of money George Simmel noted, money makes human interaction more instrumental in character and acquiring money became an end in itself. The urban life is a symbol of consumerism, something like alienation where citizens are strangers to one another. On the other hand his writing on the Philosophy of Fashion Simmel explored that with the increasing specialization of production the success of fashion came which also established identity of its producers as members of a collectivity.

The common features of all four classical sociological theorists are that their theories reflected a sort of tension during modernity although they were also aware of the advantages of the modernity.

As mentioned before modernity also had a similar impact to transform art world.

F. Nietzsche wrote, composer Wagner's aesthetic modernity expresses declining culture which can excite weary nerves. In Nietzsche's work modernity is defined as the end of enlightenment and emergence of modern mass democracy.

In the work of French poet and critic Charles Baudelaire modernity is a period when aristocracy got weakened and democracy was on its way, a period of historical transformation. Baudelaire depicts that modernity as the fragmented nature of modern urban life within alienation is experienced.

Comparison between Indian and European Middle Class

The origin of European and Indian middle class explicit unparallel direction due to differing social system, the following discourse will unravel the matter.

Coming to argument on middle class in India, we note that westernized education system produced an educated middle class alongside the intellectual.

P.C. Joshi makes a rational comment. It should be noted that as the internal bulwark of colonial ideology and culture the British tried to promote the growth of an anglicized middle class through modern education in colonial universities.

But the major difference between western intellectual and the Indian is that some portion of the western intellectuals criticized the shift (pre-industrial to industrial society) while the intellectuals of India rather remain passive and silent followers of capitalist social order.

Secondly, European middle class and bourgeois significantly contributed to the advancement of technological society.

Indian middle class merely followed the ideology of social transformation into colonial capitalism. They perceived myth of European people and their culture more advanced particularly the community whose background was not linked with feudal nobility. But to some extent the descendant of Indian nobility also became the follower of western culture. Many colonial rulers eagarly attended dance parties arranged by the Muslim nobility.

Thirdly, bourgeois of the Western Europe in time of social change gained enormous influence in society. But in India, a particular portion of middle class became interested in power. Tara Chand said that European middle class composed merchant industrialist as well as intellectual. On the contrary, Indian middle class had its roots in the agrarian system.

Fourthly, a portion of Indian middle class comprised cultural activists and literary giants. To mention a few writers from Bengal Bankim, Sharat Chandra, Tagore, Nazrul whose greatest concern was to retain cultural identity and to raise awareness against colonialism.

In case of India, prolonged British rule as external power converted India into an agricultural hinterland of British imperialism. Cultural activities in pre-independence India by cultural activists like musicians, dancers, novelists and others played a vital role in building a national identity.

> ... Cultural activity then was also not just a matter of providing mere entertainment or recreation to the Indian people. It had a political and ethical significance. (Joshi, 1996: p. 6)

What is evident is that a portion of Indian middle class was the product of westernized education system and newly emerged middle class never raised voice against the journey of capitalism. Professor A.K. Nazmul Karim wrote about rising middle class during transition of European society in his words:

> In the western set-up we find that at the initial stages of the development of capitalism the bourgeoisie constituted the middle class. This was because the bourgeoisie was the owner of the new health arising out of capitalist accumulation but the feudal class continued to the possessor of the higher social status arising out of the traditional bases on land control. In such a situation the bourgeoisie constituted the middle class. However, the members of the rising bourgeoisie gradually attained their social status by having marital and such other social ties with the members of the feudal class who were the hereditary possessors of social status. Things are different now. The bourgeoisie today constitutes the upper class as the finance capitalist. He enjoys the highest social status and middle class is the petite bourgeoisie.

Whatever the nature of both the societies, the important point is that India alongside Europe confronted the wave of modernity.

In Europe who considered new social system (capitalism) as hindrance to old social order belonged to English literary critic and the scholars of Frankfurt school. All the scholars advocated high culture and blamed mass media as the provider of inferior culture by standardization and mass scale production to cater to inferior audiences. Mathew Arnold, T.S. Eliot, F.R. Leavis, John Ruskin dreamed of a national culture and remarked on media as the promoter of mass, semi-literate people culture. In India the middle class emerged from traditional background and most of them worked in favor of change instead of transmitting the tradition. It will be no exaggeration to comment that one section of the intellectuals remained in orthodoxy in the guise of modernism.

Although many elements like rationality, secularism, democracy, rational judicial, administrative system was derived from the West but rigidity in caste system, irrationality in bureaucratic form is observed to some extent. M.N. Shrinivas comments that tradition went hand in hand during modernization process. The rise of nationalism, new political system, incorporation of innovative science and technology, Western education system all these aspects came in India as a result of 150 years of British rule. Shrinivas has not considered modernity in Indian soil as an independent variable.

Indian social thinker Y. Singh commented that the process of modernization in Indian society made significant impact on agriculture and industry but cultural modernization still awaited on the problem of social justice and poverty.

However the role of middle class is a matter of academic debate for some valid reasons.

Dipankar Gupta has sketched about middle class in contemporary India:

> "Their commitment to principles of democracy is weak. It thrives on connections, family and patronage. Instead of animating public institutions, members of this class are constantly undermining them with their allegiance to norms of patronage. Instead of pursuing individualism, as the western middle class did, the Indian middle class is an ardent advocate of privilege."

What is apparent is that Indian middle class lacks in distinctive features.

2

Culture: A Comparative Discourse

Defining culture is one of the critical issues in cultural theory. Before the decade 1940, the concept of culture was confined to the meaning and understanding of higher literature, classical music, fine arts and aesthetic analysis. Mathew Arnold, John Ruskin, F.R. Leavis used the term culture to mean these special fields and by cultured human beings they included those who had the pursuit of perfection in these specialized subjects. But after 1950 the interpretation of culture widened as British cultural studies broke off to conceive culture from elitist viewpoint.

Richard Hoggart and R. Williams experienced that so called notion of culture as a realm of beauty of forms was confronting new standard by the value that emerged from the working class, which Eliot and Leavis termed cultural decline. Both Hoggart and Williams put mass culture and working class culture on the academic discourse.

> The old forms of culture are in danger of being replaced by a poorer kind of classless... culture ... and this is to be regretted (Hoggart, 1958: p. 343).

Not only to examine social, political situation or economic issue in the realm of cultural theory but to theorize culture within the spheres of Literature, Art, Music and the concept of modernity. Modern industrialism was viewed in many different ways by the social thinkers. From Karl Marx to Max Weber, Gramsci or the Frankfurt school and their Theories noticeably differ from one another in approach. Of these various perspectives the Frankfurt school had laid the foundation of critical Theories. Critical thinkers have made us to understand why changes take place in material or non-material culture. The available definition of culture is many. However Karl Marx viewed culture in terms of ideology, power and economic life. To Marx culture reflects interest of the ruling class and business giants. Max Weber saw culture in relation to human actions shaped by religious belief to attain material success. Antonio Gramsci viewed culture in terms of hegemonic belief or dominant cultural Principles. In Frankfurt school scholars concern about the negative effect of technology, pessimistic view about popular culture and its impact on social life. Its scholars' attempt to make understand the value of high culture and the underlying motive in popular culture in particular. Frankfurt school scholars Adorno and Horkheimer viewed capitalist culture as an instrument of oppression and exploitation. Of critical thinkers, particularly mostly Neo-Marxian intellectuals of Frankfurt school are critical to mass culture. A mass is a set of people who share some common objects but it is not compulsory that people must have physical presence. The phenomenon of mass is the outcome of modern technological revolution.

However, Marxian intellectual Gramsci seems to have adopted a compromising outlook on culture. He placed emphasis on popular culture based on folklore. His view on popular culture is written below:

> The simple truth is that various forms of folklore combining with simple tune and rhythm are popularly known as folksong or rhythmic poetry and proverb. All are tied with everyday life of rural people because these cultural contents have potential to make understand the common folks about the complex world.

Similar view about popular culture was matter of academic research in The Center for Contemporary Cultural Studies led by Stuart Hall at the Birmingham University (England) during the 1960s. Most of the theorists came from lower social classes. The theorists advocated for popular culture and criticized elite domination in society. They defended indigenous forms of popular culture as an expression of minority group. The theorists of British cultural studies value and empower minorities and their culture. Limitations of some British cultural studies is a direct involvement of British social movements e.g. feminism, youth movements, racial and ethnic movements and British Labours party factions. The theorists ignore approach of objectivity in their research. As a consequence, their research works do not serve the aims of science. On the opposite pole, the Frankfurt school viewed capitalist mode of production and its relation to production as the coordinator of mass culture, which undermined avant-garde (high culture) culture. T. Adorno viewed music in terms of other social forces. His critique of works about composers like Wagner, Beethoven, Schoenberg, and Stravinsky indicates that the field of music also gives direction of social change. His work in association with M. Horkheimer Dialectic of Enlightenment and single-handed work Philosophy of Modern Music is considered to be a pioneering work about Sociology of Music. In the theory of culture industry Adorno and Horkheimer blamed American media to have monopoly over supply of entertainment with overly production of pop culture. In his later work he expounded that Schoenberg's music represents progressive force-application of twelve-tone technique. On many writings about Wagner, Adorno noted Wagner's deviation of aesthetic in the grip of mass demand and business interest turned his music helpless prey of situation; in other words an antithesis of arts responsibility on the philosophical question of 'art for art's sake.'

On the other hand, Adorno's critique explores that Wagner's compromise with culture industry by aesthetic backwardness is a synthesis with his own time. Compared to the West cultural modernism in Indian soil, particularly the domain of music does not reveal similar pace as Indian literature had great influence after the process of the European contact but influences caused by the modernity in the realm of traditional music obviously deserve attention i.e. notation system in oral tradition, use of recorder in *guru-shishya parampara*, orchestra of western classical music in film industry. Later on A.I.R. speak of principle of modernity applied on traditional musical culture to some extent.

The Frankfurt school scholar Leo Lowenthal argues that a product of popular culture has none of the features of genuine art but in all its media popular culture proves to have its own genuine characteristics: standardization, stereotypy, conservatism, mendacity, manipulated consumer goods.

However, all the critical Theorists and their theme on mass culture was propounded on some assumptions:

- Mass culture is pleasure oriented.
- Mass culture has reduced aesthetic standard.
- Mass culture transforms creators into workers at the cost of giving up individual skill.
- Mass culture is produced in keeping with profit motive.
- Mass culture concedes domination of technological society.

Finally, popular culture is blamed for lower taste audience culture. Before I start the discourse about the differences between high culture and popular culture, I feel it necessary a bird's eye view on taste because taste determines individual's appreciation of cultural products that he/she will choose.

What is Taste?

Taste can be explained as aesthetic attention. In this consideration every person has certain taste. But aesthetic value may differ from person to person on the ground of variation in attention, perception on any artwork or a piece of artwork.

The values and standards constitute the basis of what I define as a taste culture. It is the ideology that aggregates of particular taste culture reveal similar choices. But in reality taste may vary within the same taste culture people.

Therefore, the term taste can be conceived as aesthetic attitude. An attitude organizes and directs our awareness of the world. The aesthetic attitude is not the attitude, which people usually adopt. The attitude, which is customarily taken, can be called the attitude of practical perception.

A musician of higher form usually refuses to attend pop concert, a performer of light music may listen to classical music to some extent at private place but does not usually attend classical music concert. The former has responsibility to aesthetic standard, the latter feel obligation to the demand of the market.

Therefore, what is apparent is that aesthetic attitude indicates the goal of person's liking, associated with goal oriented activity. Persons with little perception about Indian *raga* may not appreciate a *Khayal* in popular *raga*, but conceive a film song based on that *raga* as classic. Aesthetic attitude is also related to person's degree of aesthetic knowledge. This is the key reason that mass public are unable to understand higher music.

Taste Culture

Diversity about aesthetic standard and values make different taste culture as well as different taste audiences.

> Taste culture is not a cohesive value system and taste public are not organized groups; the former are aggregates of similar values and usually but not always similar content and the latter are aggregates of people with usually but not always similar values making similar choices from the available offerings of culture. Moreover, they are analytic aggregates, which are constructed by the social researcher. (Gans, 1974, pp. 69-70)

The literary meaning of taste culture is confined to elite culture or high culture. Taste culture reflects cultural form like higher music, art, literature, sculpture, drama and so forth and value judgement of these forms by the significant part of the society. But it is noticeable that lay public also intend to pass value judgement of higher culture. On the contrary, the conservative scholar's popular culture is created for the masses that comprise of half educated or illiterate, low-income population. There remains one major quest, which is the creator of high culture or popular culture? High culture creators include serious artiste/artist, writer etc. Popular culture creators are considered to be semi-trained, amateur creators. Various media on different cultural policy give exposure of these cultures.

Taste Structure

Artistic activities do not take place in vacuum rather it eventuates in a network of artistic production since a creator needs audience and audience also feel a need for enjoyment of creation, both are essential features of artistic production. Cultural practices are collective behavior. Although cultural activities combine auxiliary classes but social location of the cultural agents also express individual taste to some extent.

But Paul Lazarsfeld attempted to break away the distinction between cultural choices on the basis of class structure.

On the other hand, P. Bourdieu correlated taste in terms of class position. In Bourdieu's three-folded taste classification i.e. legitimate taste is related with aesthetic disposition, widespread in the educated sections of the dominant class while the middle brow taste means taste of the middle class and popular taste prevalent in the working class.

To Bourdieu artistic competence is associated with aesthetic disposition, which is a form of knowledge. Artistic competence enables the beholder to situate the work of art in relation to the universe of the artistic possibilities of which it is a part.

Popular artwork is obliged to various categories of consumers with a view to transactions and compromise with market demand.

Higher art which belongs to the field of restricted production in Bourdieu's terminology produce for other producers (the artist/artiste, benefactors etc.). Here, the expectation of making profit is excluded. This field discredits the field of large scale productions because higher art considerably dominates the field of culture. For instance, the investment of popular culture goes to privately owned television, cinematic production, inferior music, mass produced literature and the like.

In an essay 'Distinction' Bourdieu argues:

> Whereas the ideology of charisma regards taste in legitimate culture as a gift of nature, scientific observation shows that cultural needs are the product of upbringing and education. Surveys establish that all cultural practices (museum visits, concert going, reading etc.) and preferences in literature, painting or music, are closely linked to educational level (measure by qualification or length of schooling) and secondarily to social origin.

> The relative weight of home background and of formal education (the effectiveness and duration of which are closely dependent on social origin) varies according to the extent to which the different cultural practices are recognized and taught by the educational system and the influence on social origin is strongest other things being equal in extra-curricular and Avant-garde culture. To the socially recognized hierarchy of the arts and within each of them, of genres, schools or periods corresponds a social hierarchy of the consumers. This predisposes tastes to function as markers of 'class.'

Bourdieu conceived taste as a dimension of broader *habitus*. Bourdieu's goal was to attack the philosophical belief that aesthetic judgements are built on objective, universal criteria about what was in good or bad taste.

According to Bourdieu the aesthetics of pure taste are based on a refusal of impure taste. By impure taste Bourdieu meant that particular taste which is related to the pleasure of the senses.

I have an interest to interpret Indian musical field through Bourdieu's model of culture.

During Renaissance in India the value of western education and its implication made literary intellectuals whose work revealed westernized model of literature.

Poetry and literature in Bengal had gone through two distinct stages and seem to be preparing for a third of which one cannot foresee the character. It began with European and mostly the English influence, says Sri Aurobindo. Bourdieu's link between education and developing taste has similar value in India. The rise of British rule changed the conditions of existing land system through permanent settlement. This structural shift had effected to lessen the power of some existing nobility of that time. For instance, Nawab Wazid Ali Shah of Lucknow was deposed as ruler but he made a mentionable musical ambience with court musicians to Metiaburuz outside Calcutta. This example indicates that downward social position has nothing to do with change in taste or once a particular cultural taste achieved may continue in later life. Crisis in life situation may not cause degradation of individual's taste.

Secondly, Bourdieu's measuring of high taste, as symbol of status is also applicable into Indian history of music; for example, in the late nineteenth century the newly rising business class would listen to classical music and would arrange musical soiree for attaining status by showing taste for higher music.

Therefore, we observe that P. Bourdieu's empirical focus on French society has some value in the Indian societal context. But survey result, which is based on a particular social group, cannot be significant about society as a whole. Many persons at the same time may have embodied plural taste. Taste is not even equally distributed in family members i.e. parents have taste for traditional culture but their children may develop taste for Western popular culture through media or availability of cassettes, CDs, videos etc.

Further, contemporary Indian middle class reveals tendency to follow contradictory cultural values. Most of its members to be modern in their own sense follow fashion, style and choices of music in the measure of western popular culture. On the other hand, they reveal rigid attitude to maintain traditional social institutions such as caste, family, marriage. Therefore, the path of Indian middle class exists in between traditional and borrowing culture.

Cultural mobility may remain unaffected despite social mobility occurs. When ordinary people are striving for upper mobility through professional attainment their taste may turn towards material culture, for instance, building a better house, buying a car but when the question comes about higher music and any higher art they remain in their original taste; in other words they display taste for low culture.

As a matter of fact, binary of culture by naming legitimate and illegitimate distinction, the elite of French society advocated high culture as refined intellectual, enduring, and the contrast popular culture as trivial, conducive to the working class taste. What is evident is that taste for higher culture was used as power in French society.

I have adopted two different dimensions to work on high culture and popular culture i.e. the relation of both the culture from aesthetic viewpoint and social structure as well.

High Culture Versus Popular Culture

- High culture situates in autonomous field. Since the production of this field enjoys much freedom hence the producers care little about making profit.
- Higher culture tends to be obliged to aesthetic standard; hence its creators enjoy power over the creators of heterogeneous cultural producers. Popular culture content contains surface aesthetic elements, as a consequence its popularity is not guaranteed for a long time.
- Many creations of higher culture may fail to gain appreciation in contemporary era. But it may regain its value after some time. For example, paintings of Van Gogh received appreciation after his demise. But contents of popular culture if not accepted in current time may be forgotten forever. Therefore, sometimes investment in popular culture may cause acute loss on the part of the investor.
- Higher culture maintains critics for value judgements. Criticism is published in newspaper or cultural magazines with a view that criticism should be accepted by the creator, organizer, and other agents of cultural production. Many a time critics receive negative response from the creators since there remains gap between critics' understanding and the way artiste created. On the contrary information about popular culture and its contents that are expressed in different media and newspaper talk about basically business imperative. Box office opinion is given top priority in popular culture.
- Higher culture artistes/artists are highly trained; on the other hand, popular culture singers excel in popular art. They are basically amateur and their practices of

music are confined to its group members whereas the group members pass value judgement on the creation. Success depends on box office rating.

- Higher culture is creator oriented, that is why its audiences view work of art from creator's viewpoint. Here, audiences are smaller than popular culture audience. Popular culture is almost aloof from moral responsibility to aesthetic standard. In popular entertainment fare like soap opera, movies, the question of higher philosophical issues and its value stand secondary and gratification of the public is given top priority. The production aims at reaching out the largest possible average audiences.
- Popular culture is blamed for borrowing contents from higher culture. Bollywood movie *Hum Dil De Chuke Sanam* and its music in *raga Ahir Bhairo al bela sajan aao ri* is a composition of *Hindustani* classical music. Performer's representation of the composition may be objectionable to master's musician due to breaking of norms of *khayal* singing. Nevertheless, in one sense, high culture artistes enjoy privilege. Tendencies to borrow elements from popular form by many higher culture creators are also evident. Painter Picasso borrowed elements, techniques from African art. In India many a number of artistes sing infusing distinctive elements of various *Gharanas* to receive attention from all types of audience. The question remains: is classical music duly creator oriented?
- Having a small size audience high culture enjoys more prestige than popular culture. High culture subjects are taught in prestigious universities, on the other hand popular culture is taught in privately established institution or media institute run by private sectors, sometimes funded by government to a lesser extent.
- It is believed that popular culture receives attention through publicity and does not maintain critics but in

America popular culture critics also receive greater value by the media professional to express their opinions. American folk singer Bob Dylan started his career with civil right song, political song in 1960s. Later with electric guitar songs he composed was named Rock N Roll but critics analyzed his song as Folk Rock. In recent era popular form like *Bhangra* or others that popular song singers have named Indi pop but critics in India are not very vocal. Therefore, we notice that in India freedom of cultural activities is more than other parts of the world.

- In an era of globalization popular culture is being consumed beyond boundaries without limit. Now the field has got its own set of critics who act as publicists. In apparent contrast most critics of classical music in India harbour negative attitude towards artistes and their performance.
- When professional critics attack successful popular culture creators for their failure to meet high culture standards, they defend themselves saying public are their strength. The creators, producers of this culture care for little about desirability of taste audience.
- On the contrary high culture creators during rise in the world of art value criticism a lot. But when they achieve support of the audience care little about whatever the critics write.
- Popular culture has been considered as entertaining merely. But many a time an innovative popular culture creator and his creation may draw attention for all taste people, for example, Disney land. In contrast, many a time high culture remains indebted to folk culture but competent musicians often keep silence about borrowing. Likewise some high culture composers have borrowed elements from Jazz music and folk music in the west. They do not verbally acknowledge that for fear of degrading status.

- Both popular culture and high culture content can be political. *Dhrupad* was sung in praise of political elite and aristocracy. Rock music by the rock musicians also accelerated to overthrow the communist government from the East Germany.
- From recent studies scholarly communities voice that popular music has adopted the notion of noise because noise has power to be heard. Noise and loudness in musical production also function similarly. It engages attention, for instance, sound signals, traffic whistles, thus, loud sound becomes associated with power. Likewise many *Hindustani* classical performers have incorporated this idea of loudness. Particularly followers of *Gwalior gharana* prefer to produce volatile execution of voice.
- High culture critics hold a little dominance over its creators in India. In India classical musician often reshapes after hearing comments of the audience or fellow musicians. Because criticism in India did not keep pace with the critics of western countries for lack of professionalism. In the west high culture critic's evaluations are considered seriously by its creators.
- In classical music materials are complex enough and it requires training and practice to demonstrate. It strictly maintains theoretical rules. In contrast, Indian film music although its root lies in Indian tone but application of western harmony in background music sometimes sounds strange to traditional listeners. Female singers select high scale to assert that they have got high pitched voice. Western film song singer's voice production seems to be more or less natural since they follow scale according to ability of vocal.
- The mass culture critics have been charged by the opposition, radical thinkers that they are the defenders only. Apart from literary critics of the west, their music and art critics also hold much prestigious position in

the west than it is in India. Critics are supported by the academics with great importance in the west.

- High culture audiences take pride on their taste. Popular culture audience is not concerned with prestige the high culture audiences possess. They are concerned with entertainment other than cultural prestige.
- In popular culture, its creators confront more conflict over the issue if its contents are to be reached to the total audience. In India in the field of music its organizers allow the public to attend concert, conferences, incapable of purchasing tickets. They rather face conflict if selected artistes' performance would cater to the public. Comparatively, in democratic India consumption and creation is more democratic. But in the west attending on opera or symphony concert audience require high fees ticket.
- This shows that unlike the west, higher music of India has not been commercially successful. In India corporate sponsors classical concerts seek to improve public relations by means of pass. Not all corporate are really admirer of higher music but their motive lies in status seeking and product promotion.

To summarize, historically high culture played a dominant role in society. Apart from high culture, folk culture also contributed to the gratification of ordinary folks. High culture confronted challenge by popular culture with the origin of technological society. The bottom line is popular music or other popular art is the voice of the masses but not without the presence of technology. Its contents are produced to sale merely. To tell the truth the struggle of critics of mass culture reveals power over commercial culture. Thus the upholders of high culture became reactionary over commercial culture due to overemphasis of propagation. However, thinking of intellectuals certainly has got significant value to cultural policy makers. Undoubtedly popular culture panders to culturally illiterate commoners. It is an opposition to critical cultural values, in relation to creativity. But it is not my intention to charge popular culture aimlessly. The point to note here is that it is aesthetically poor.

This discourse from various paradigms is an effort to search answer changes in material as well as non-material culture. In case of India modernity movement occurred by the influence of external force. But in Europe the seed was rooted within the society to develop.

3

Style in Relation to Forms

The background of any artwork lies in the drive of forming beauty and expressiveness. At the beginning of social life some human beings attempted to sublimate emotions through creative disposition. Some attempted to express feelings through language and writing, some through colour, earth, stone, while the others adopted sound. From the medium of language literature evolved, colour and line constituted Fine arts and sound and notes (*Swaras*) constituted the base of Music. What is apparent is that elements and presentation of artwork differ from one art medium to another. Moreover, feelings, introspection, thinking and presentation of any piece of musical work differ from artiste to artiste. The originality of any artistic form depends on the way an artiste/artist employs technique, material to give a defined shape or expressiveness. The concept of style is nothing new in analysis of artwork. The application of the term style came in use to mean writing style; in other words the way a writer expresses his/her feeling by the use of language. In course of time the term style gradually entered in Fine arts, Drama, Sculpture and Music as well. Style in European literature has two main streams: one is platonic and another is influenced by the opinion of Aristotle. Aristotle and Kant and all other philosophers had reached the consensus that the objective of literature is to give life and idea into concrete form. However subject matter of painting or sculpture is visible, but what art music represents is basically an abstract feeling. Through the medium of sound an artiste reveals basically those feelings, which literature, painting or other arts may not adequately express. In the history of Indian music various forms evolved from time to time, wherein individual artiste's selection of notes, combination of notes, selection of tempo, choice of composition, presentation of *ragas* distinguishes from one artiste to another. Here lies the key question of musical style. The characteristics incorporated with particular elements to create any piece of artwork or particular form is called style. Distinctive style of vocal or instrumental music made the ground of *Gharanas*. Artistes have been demonstrating *ragas* in different forms over the centuries. The same *ragas* appear diversifying by the listeners because of differences in representation of *raga* or treatment artistes make. *Dhrupad* and *Khayal* two pure forms are distinguished from each other in consideration of style.

Style constitutes the universe of discourse within which musical meaning arises. There are many musical styles. They vary from culture to culture, from epoch within the same culture, and even within the same epoch and culture. This plurality of musical styles results because styles exist not as psychological processes ingrained as habits in the perceptions, dispositions, and responses of those who have learned through practice and experience to understand a particular style. What remains constant from style to style are not scales, modes, harmonies, or manners of performance, but the psychology of human mental processes the ways in which the mind, operating within the context of culturally established norms, selects and organizes the stimuli that are presented to it. For instance, the human mind, striving for stability and completeness, "expects" structural gaps to be filled in. But what constitutes a structural gap will vary from style to style. (Meyer, 1967, p.7).

Dhrupad

It is said that fifteenth and sixteenth centuries were the golden age for *Dhrupad*. *Dhrupad* is a classical form, which consists of four parts: *sthayi, antara, bhog* and *abhog*. *Dhrupad* singing maintains a detailed *aalap* with nom, tom which have no literary meaning but it creates a rhythmic pattern. *Aalap* moves in slow, medium and faster tempo. In *aalap* portion *meed, kan, aandolon, gamaka* are used to give musical expression. In the performance of *bandish bol*-phrases or using the song words with rhythmic variation provide a grave feature of the classical form. Pakhawaj is an accompanying instrument of *dhrupad* singing. In musical sphere the term style is associated with two parts: namely (*a*) composer (*b*) the artiste; the composer creates *bandishes* and the performer gives practical rendition. At times the composer and the performer happen to be the same artiste. For example, Tansen sang mostly his own composition. The style of *Dhrupad* singing evolved with elaboration of *aalap* where a performer attempts to define the *raga* from slow medium to faster tempo in combination of four parts.

From the writing of *Ain-e-Akbari* it is known that in fifteenth and sixteenth century Gwalior became a suitable place where many musicians found the appreciation of their art. The kings of Tomar dynasty ruled Gwalior almost hundred years. Among the kings of this dynasty Mansingh Tomar deserves special mention.

Raja Mansingh Tomar (1486-1519) was a musicologist and a great patron of music. He is credited with the introduction of *Dhruvapada*, which is basically an improvised and modified form of *Dhruva*, a kind of *Prabandha* form, which was prevalent during 8th or 9th century A.D. Raja Mansingh assembled a great number of Nayakas (musician and musicologist as well) in his court. From Faqirullah's *'Raga Darpan'* it is known that Nayaka Bakshu, Nayaka Bhannu, Pandaviya and many others were Tomar's court musicians. Musical soiree was an everyday affair in King's court. Two great musicians Nayaka Baija and Nayaka Bakshu provided assistance in composing many *Dhruvapadas*. With the assistance of Pandaviya and other musicians Raja Mansingh Tomar compiled the book *Manakutuhala*. The original *Manakutuhala* is not available now-a-days. Faqirullah's *Raga Darpana* is the translation of *Manakutuhala* in Persian language. But Dr. Thakur Jaideva disagrees on the point that since in the first chapter, Faqirullah himself admitted that he had added some of his own writing in the book, therefore, it will not be justified to say that *Raga Darpana* is the accurate translation of *Manakutuhala*.

Raja Mansingh who composed *Dhrupad* bears characteristically the evidence of that particular period and the taste of the listeners. There is no doubt that during the period of Raja Mansingh Tomar *Dhrupad* and its popularity reached its zenith. Abul Fazal had written that King Akbar invited artistes of various ethnic group in his court namely Irani, Turani, Kashmiri. But Tansen was the brightest star in Akbar's court. Tansen's real name was Tana Mishra and he was born as a brahmin. Tansen composed *Dhrupad* in praise of king, Maharaja and his other compositions were made to pay *bhakti* to deities and even the prophet of Islam after being a follower of Muhammad Gaus, a sufi saint. In an essay entitled *Dhrupada*: its legacy and dynamics, Sumati Mutatkar classified literary contents of *Dhrupada* as follows:

(*i*) Praise of gods and goddesses like Brahma, Mahesh, Ganesha, Hanuman, Sri Rama, Sri Krishna, Saraswati, Durga, Parvati, Lakshmi and Kali to whom invocatory hymns were addressed, similar songs in praise of Allah, Mohammad etc. A subsidiary category would be songs intimately addressed to the deity, especially Lord Krishna and songs extolling the importance and varieties of *bhakti* (devotion), moral virtues like truth, love and compassion.

(*ii*) Praise of royal patrons, extolling their valour, generosity and greatness.

(*iii*) Nayaka-nayika theme songs depicting the eight nayikas detailed in Sanskrit poetics. Description of female beauty and erotic themes also belong to this category.

(*iv*) Nada-brahman themes also belong to this category. The scope and terminology of music embodied in shastric lore.

(*v*) Beauties of nature songs depicting seasons like spring, rainy season and summer.

Baani in *Dhrupad* singing has special meaning. Distinctive style of composition and rendition in *Dhrupad* singing is called *baani*. Tansen is said to have introduced *Gaurhara baani*.

Khandar baani was introduced by Samokhan Singh. Two other *baanis* namely *Dagur baani* by Brijchandra, *Nauhara baani* by Shrichand were introduced in times of King Akbar. Abul Fazal had mentioned that Tansen by his first performance delighted such a way that King Akbar gave him two lakh rupees. But popularity of anyone or any form is not guaranteed for unlimited time.

In fact, one cannot even say for sure that any musical style will be appealing in all ages.

If a style does not develop and change, it necessarily decays and dies (Meyer, 1967, p. 105).

The concept of musical style, in turn, leads directly to another concept of style period. A style period may be defined simply as the period of time in which certain style elements dominate.

Genesis of Khayal

The general meaning of *Khayal* is imagination or thought. Whatever the meaning of *Khayal*, this is the most popular Hindustani form even today. This vocal form represents *raga* music. In the middle of the eighteenth century the popularity of *Dhrupad* started to decline and *Khayal* as a rising form came into the light. After the demise of Tansen, kings and nobles became more interested in *Khayal* rather than *Dhrupad*. There remains much controversy concerning the originator of *Khayal*. Some musicologists credit Hussain Shah Sharqi while the others credit Sadarang as the originator of *Khayal*.

Sultan Hussain Shah Sharqi the last king of Tughlak dynasty invented *Kalavanti Khayal*, a form called *chutkala* prevalent in his time was turned into a form of *Khayal*. Perhaps, it was not appealing to the audience for a long time. Therefore, *Khayal* remained in the stage of stasis. A style may encounter degeneration due to lack of discerning audiences. But to Meyer degeneration also refers a kind of change.

During Renaissance in India, *Khayal* appeared as an autonomous artistic form free from political slogan. In nineteenth century Indian Music like Europe also had been undergoing the process of autonomy. Sadarang or Niamat Khan was a musician

(Veen player) under the Emperor Mohammad Shah of Delhi. According to the scholar musicologist Sadarang was a descendent of Tansena. But his parentage remains still in the dark. Pandit V.N. Bhatkhande said that Lala Khan was his father. The other opinion claims that Dargaha Kuli Khan was his father.

A widely prevalent story in musicology is that once Sadarang was ordered to play *Vina* with a *Dhrupad* singer. In such case he refused emperor's order and left the court. Later he devoted himself in *Khayal* practice and imparted knowledge to his disciples. Sadarang's *Khayal* had distinct influence of *Dhrupada*.

Sumati Mutatkar writes thus: The *dhrupada* based slow *khayal* came up only in the early 18th century and gained wider currency. Renowned exponents of *dhrupada* and *vina* like Niyamat Khan Sadarang and his nephew Feroz Khan Adarang, musicians at the court of Mohammad Shah Rangile, devised a slow moving structure for *khayal*, retaining the *raga* features and stateliness of *dhrupada*, partially freeing it from rhythmic rigidity. With a much smaller text in a more colloquial language and with more attractive ornamentation and technique, this *khayal*, an offshoot of *dhrupada*, offered many new avenues of musical expression.

Sadarang composed hundreds of *khayal* bandishes that are still popular. He introduced *sthayi* and *antara* as two parts of *Khayal*. Now-a-days the subject of *khayal* bandishes still follows the ideology of Sadarang. Many Khayalias follow basically Sadarang's *Khayal*. After Sadarang introduced *Khayal* it remained popular over the centuries and *Dhrupada* went for stasis stage.

A stasis might last for three or four generations according to Meyer. However various *gharanas* of *khayal* singing follow distinctive style. But every authentic *gharana* strictly abides by some common theories of *khayal* presentation.

These are briefly,

- Technique of voice production or use of voice
- The pattern of composition/*bandish*
- Use of *laya* (tempo)
- Particular style of *raga bistar* (elaboration)

- Choice of *raga*
- Presentation of *tanas*

We may now examine salient features of some parent *gharanas* in brief.

Delhi Gharana

- Charming pattern in *aalap*
- *Tanas* like *Jod, Tod ke tana, Jhoola ke tanas, Ukhad ke tanas,* etc. (Mukherjee, 1989, p. 59)
- *Khayal* singing in uncommon, mixed *ragas* like *Anand Sri, Langkeshri* etc. Sometimes mixed *ragas* e.g. *Hindol bahar, Nayaki kanada, Shahana Malhar* etc.
- Selection of uncommon *talas* and excellent command in tempo

Gwalior Gharana

- Volatile execution of voice
- Style of *raga aalap* is based on straight pattern
- Emphasis on *sapat tana*
- *Boltanas*
- Application of *gamaka* etc.

Jaipur Gharana

- *Bistar* of *khayal* has influence of *dhrupada.*
- Compositions are set to brief mode.
- *Madhyalaya khayal.* Expert artistes are capable of executing *vakra tanas* and *layakari tanas.*

Agra Gharana

The basic features as under:

- Preface of *aalap/nom tom* in *Dhrupad* style followed by *Dhamar.*
- *Dhrupad* based *vilambit khayals*
- Exquisite *Drut khayals* with brilliant *bolkari*; excellent use of *boltans.*
- Bold and powerful voice and *tanas* with heavy and clear beats. (Mukherjee, 1989, p. 63)

Kirana Gharana

- *Aalap* in slow tempo, improvisation of *aalap* in gradual progression of notes.
- Intricate *sargam* pattern.
- *Tanas* built in consistent manner and use of *gamaka tanas*.
- Not all but ustad like Abdul Karim Khan sang *Thumri* besides *khayal*.
- Intonation and emotional content is considered two most important features here.

...extent of style is a function of the cultural ideological environment in which it exists. In some cultures intra-stylistic changes have been slow or after a particular level of complexity is reached, virtually non-existent; there is stasis. (ibid, p.122)

But stasis does not mean that the musical system will be lost forever. Some musicians may still keep hold the system despite demand decreases. After centuries many artistes sing *Dhrupad* in recent years. This means that taste for *Dhrupad* singing is rising again.

Now the question arises why *Khayal* became popular? *Khayal* especially Sadarang's *Khayal* follows faster *tana, gamaka tana*. *Dhrupad* and its *gamaka* retain slower tempo. In *khayal* freedom for graces is allowed. The *aalapa* of *Khayal* is more improvised. In *vilambit khayal* singing *aalap* is rendered in different *talas* i.e. *ektal*, *jhumra* etc. *Sargam* gives graces in *khayal* singing but this important element is completely absent in *Dhrupada* singing. In *khayal* singing a *khayalia* retains rhythm in *vilambit aalap*. After *aalap sargam* in various tempo differs from artiste to artiste in various *gharanas*. The last portion of *vilambit khayal* singing is *gamaka*. An artiste needs much practice to mature *gamaka*. All these components comprise *vilambit khayal*. The *chotta khayal* maintains faster tempo. Artistes usually select *tintal*, *jhaptal*, *drut ektal*, *adachautal* etc. according to individual taste. The mass audience takes *chotta khayal* with great enthusiasm. *Madhyalaya khayal* is diversity in *khayal* singing.

Vocalists like Pandit Aloke Chatterjee, Ustad Iqbal Ahmed Khan and many others have excelled in *khayal* of this type. Duration of *madhyalaya khayal* ranges from fifteen to twenty minutes. What is clear is that in *Khayal* artistes enjoy freedom of improvisation to show vocal skill with the power of imagination. Moreover in the evolution of style a certain time arrives where prevalent form does not attract the audiences. Not only this, creative artistes also try to remain innovative. Therefore, it is practically impossible to keep style static, for the creative ones and for creative enterprise.

Dynamism is natural in style. Therefore, a change in style does not necessarily mean that previous style is inferior. Beauty in music acts beyond boundaries. To create beauty in music some artistes may go for experiment, which has a satiable effect on the part of the creator even for the receptors. Author Binata Maitra claims that societal and environmental changes are the reason for the emergence of *Khayal* and its style. In my opinion, there is no link between social change and style change. When *Khayal* was on the spotlight, another form named *tappa* also came into the light. From feudal socio-economic and colonial political structure in Democratic India *khayal* is sung and heard with zeal. Different *gharanas* and its die hard followers have maintained the style of music founded by the founder. There is also ample example that a few artistes who have learnt from two or three *gharanas* later on developed a *gayaki* (The style that bears evidence of individual talent). But most public hardly has knowledge about musical style. This subject is very much scholarly and academic issue. Through performance cum demonstration master musicians can make a laudable effort to make the public understand what style is. But most musicians feel that it is needless since they wish to live in appreciation of trained ear listeners.

Taraana

The term *taraana* derives from Persian language meaning song. There is a general idea among musicians that *taraana* compositions have no meaning; meaningless words depend upon the rhythm and note pattern. In fact *taraana* is a type of *khayal* presentation of Hindustani vocal music. According to Dr. Thakur Jaideva Singh *taraana* was invented by Amir Khusraw. Dr. Singh writes that Amir Khusraw made two innovations in his *taraana*. Firstly, he used Persian words of soft consonants. Secondly he arranged these words that bore some sense. As it has been mentioned before that *taraana* words have no literary meaning. But Dr. Singh has given some examples of meaningful words used in *taraana*.

These word meanings are given below:

Dānī	You know; thou knowest (Persian)
yālā lā	A short form of yā Allah (O God)
yā lā lī	Indicative of yā Ali
Derena	An imitation of the Persian word, *derīnah*, meaning experienced
Diyā	Meaning gave (Hindi)
Nadir	A Persian word meaning unique
Tom	A Hindi word meaning you

Taraana is a dynamic form in Hindustani classical music. Musicians like Ustad Nassir Hussain Khan, Ustad Amir Khan sang *taraana* with excellence to reach out to audience. Musicians according to their preference can sing two varieties of *taraana*. In one kind of *taraana* the treatment is made like that of *chotta khayal*. In another type, tempo increases considerably at the end; words are repeated to create rhythmic pattern which sometimes resemble *jhaala* (double plucking) of Sitar playing.

Tappa

Tappa is basically a folk form of Punjab. Sori Mian introduced Sanskrit language in *Tappa* singing and turned it into a classical form. In the eighteenth century Delhi and Agra were echoed by *Tappa* singing. The literary content of *Tappa* reveals mostly love. The duration of *Tappa* does not prolong like *Dhrupad* and *Khayal*. There is a little scope of *raga* elaboration in *tappa*. The application of *murki, gamaka tana* in fast speed, *gitkari, bol-tana*, *zamzama* are the features of *Tappa* singing. Its duration ranges from ten to twelve minutes. *Talas* set to *Tappa* are mainly *Punjabi* and *Maddhaman*. *Tappa* as a popular form also travelled among the Bengalis. Ramnidhi known as *Nidhibabu*, was influenced by Sori

Mian and performed *Bangla tappa*. Sori Mian's *tappas* were ornamented with skillful *tanas*. After the demise of Sori Mian and Nidhibabu the elements of *tappa* have been incorporated in other lighter forms. Today this form is not very popular still we often observe effort of few artistes to revive this form. For instance, Malini Rajurkar, Pt. Rajan, Pt. Sajan Mishra at times sing *Tappa*. But the condition of *Tappa* singing basically denotes a stage of stasis.

Thumri

The end of nineteenth century was the period of political unrest; as a consequence, community of musicians faced rapid decline of patronage caused by uncertainty in the social and world of music. Moreover, a new business class of that particular period, who did not have adequate experience of understanding pure classical form displayed their taste for semi-classical/light classical form like *Thumri*. Earlier *Thumri* singing was confined to *Baiji* class. At the beginning *ustad* or *pandit* rarely sang *Thumri* on the ground that *Baijis* were neglected by the society. Some *Baijis* of the past are Rasoolan Bai, Zohra Bai, Jaddan Bai, who had also training in Kathak dance. Gradually rigid attitude towards *thumri* broke off as Ustad Bade Gulam Ali Khan, Patiala *gharana* Abdul Karim Khan (*Kirana gharana*), Faiyaz Khan (*Agra gharana*) performed *thumri* soulfully.

The literary expression (lyrics) of *Thumri* voices love between Lord Krishna and his consort Radha and the feminine feelings, for example, yearning for beloved, fear, hope, pangs of separation, suspicion in conjugal relationship etc.

Thumri lyrics have two phases: *sthayi* and *antara*. The first phase generally consists of one line that generally depicts emotive content. *Sthayi* in general is composed in middle octave and lower octave. *Antara* on the other hand is composed in *madhya-saptak* (middle octave) to *tar-saptak* (higher octave). *Ragas* like *Bhairavi, Jogia, Sindh Bhairabi, Pilu, Gara, Tilak Kamod, Khamaj, Kirbani, Jhinjhoti, Sohini, Shiva Ranjani, Kafi, Manj Khamaj* etc. are *ragas* selected for *thumri*. *Bol banao ki thumri* and *bol-baant ki thumri* are two major types. *Bol banao ki thumri* is sung in *talas* or time measures like Jat (16 beats) Deepchandi, Kaharwa (8 beats), *Teental* (16 beats) etc. But now-a-days a very few musicians prefer to sing *thumri* in *teental.* However, after completing improvisation with *sthayi* and *antara* artistes shift to *kaharwa* with faster tempo once again return to the original *tala* whatever it is, *Jat/Deepchandi*. This style is called *laggi. Bol-baant ki thumri* is rendered in *teental*, *sitarkhani* and *jhaptala*. This particular type of *thumri* composition was composed for dance. Of *thumri* composers Lalan Piya of Farrukhabad, Bindadin Maharaj of the Lucknow *gharana* of *kathak*, Kadar Piya and Sanat Piya and their compositions are still sung by many today. Compositions of *thumries* have been constructed in *Brij*, *Bundeli*, *Bhojpuri*, *Maghi*, *Mewati*, *Marwadi*, *Bagheli* and even colloquial Hindi like *khari boli*. This means that *thumri* song text has much influence of dialect. In *thumri* singing words receive much importance because they project specific emotional colour to phrases which characterize the *thumri* and its *raga*.

There are differences of opinion about who popularized *Thumri*. Authentic musicologists credit Nawab Wajid Ali Shah of Lucknow to popularize *Thumri*. But another group of musicologists say that from *Khadi Thumri* classical *Thumri* evolved. The musicologist of this school has assumed that *thumri* singing which is in vogue now is the improvised form of *Khadi Thumri*. In *thumri* singing purity of a *raga* is not an important aspect; it is endowed with flexibility of musical expression. An artiste can execute *swaras* (notes) of similar *ragas* in a composition of *thumri. Mind, Murchana*, small *tana* in a form of embellishment are its features. As style is a vital aspect in *Khayal* singing so style also appeared in *thumri*. These various styles are namely Benarasi *thumri*, Lucknow *thumri*, Punjabi *thumri*. *Talas* of *Thumri* singing are *Jat* (8 beats), *Deepchandi* (14 beats), *Kaharwa*, *Tintal* etc.

Rita Ganguly says, *The Banaras school has specialized in integrating tappa nuances into its slow, expansive thumri treatment. The pioneering figure in Banaras-anga thumri,* who influenced and changed the complexion *of thumri* singing was Maijuddin Khan.

Lucknow style follows a faster speed. For example, *Gitkari*, *Murki* and *Krintan* are some of its features. Punjabi *thumri* employs *sudh* and *komal swaras* in successive manner; application of short ornamentation at times seems to be an assimilation from folk form. Nawab Wajid Ali Shah's patronage brought about a new era of *thumri* singing. Some immortal singers of *thumri* are Maijuddin Khan, Abdul Karim Khan, Moti Bai, Hira Bai Barodekar, Begum Akhter and so on are still inspiration in the music world.

Dadra

Dadra is a light classical form in Hindustani music system. It is lighter than *Thumri.* Its lyrical themes cover same as *thumri.* Its melodic phrases are shorter than *Thumri.* Generally *Dadra* maintains faster tempo than *thumri* and *Dadra* is composed on *Dadra, Kaharwa, Khemta, tala* etc. The term *misra* is sometimes prefixed to the name of the *raga.* A *dadra* is composed to make sense of freedom of using notes outside the *raga.*

Other Varieties of Light Classical Form

- Some folk songs and folk tune have been adopted and sung almost in the manner of *thumri* and *dadra* by the Hindustani vocalists. These forms are namely *Chaiti, Kajari, Sabaani, Jhula, Hori.* These forms depict themes of a particular season associated with human emotion. For example, *Chaiti* is performed in the month of spring, *Kajari* and *Sabaani* in the month of rain, *Jhula* depicts a swing; its lyrics mostly covers pains of conjugal life in the rainy season. *Hori* is song of spring festival of the sprinkling of coloured water.

The author of Bharatiya Ucchanga Sangeeter Riti Bibartan (Bangla) Binata Maitra pointed out that intellectuality is a factor in the development of musical forms. I also agree with this opinion. But the author commented that after the demise of Mohammad Shah particularly from 1758 internal revolution in Delhi and chaotic political atmosphere took away the audiences from understanding of pure classical form like *Dhrupad* and *Khayal.* Undoubtedly political unrest and war interrupt any sort of cultural activities. Music is no exception. Music tends to have encouraged by the community itself and receptor as well. Music looses heart at hostility in societies. But I assume that after 1758 discerning audience's taste remained intact rather it was indicating the emergence of mass audience. Break of court, Darbar musicians found new receptors among the mass and the business class.

The relationship between art and culture is one of reciprocity. Artists shape and at the same time are shaped by culture. (ibid, p. 108).

Moreover, the Princes under British rule, had been confronting trouble as a result of inability of court patronage tremendously created an unfavorable condition for those who were listeners of pure classical form.

After the discourse of all these forms in relation to social ambience a simple question may arise: why changes or new form of style emerge? Is political system or social changes having direct impact on this?

The history of Indian classical music reveals the fact that patronage by the political elites effectively contributed to the development of higher music. It is also noticeable that some political elites were musician as well. Shift in political systems can influence other social factors that have nothing to do with the changes in musical styles. But it can hamper the practice of music. The British colonial rule could not destroy Indian musical system, although the British took a little interest in the Indian musical system. From feudal social system to democratic socio-political system Indian music particularly its lyrical part of vocal music does not reveal significant changes. The lyrics of *Dhrupad* and *Khayal* denote traditional *bandishes*, belief system of medieval society. Nevertheless a few creative artists having ignored the traditional rule to sing pre-composed *bandishes* of the *gharana* he/she belongs, have composed *bandishes* of their own. But new *bandishes* receive much appreciation despite aesthetic value may not be considered as good as traditional *bandishes*. The reason behind this can be assumed that an artist learns traditional *bandishes* of particular *gharana* through *guru-shishya parampara* and oral tradition. This is the practice of this tradition that one can take pride on account of that whatever is imparted from *guru* has greater value. This gives another meaning of status of *guru* in the field of music world including musical style. So far as music and its styles are concerned the worth-mentioning factors are creativity, imagination, need for novelty, individual talent, differences in talent; appreciation of a particular form in a given historical time is also responsible for the birth of new forms. Stagnation of some forms is responsible for change in taste, receptions, after all benefaction.

At the end of debate a few key points are to note:

It is apparent that stories occupy certain space in the literature of Indian music. The reason lies in medieval age commoners did not gain access in court cultural activities; on the other hand, for lack of journalism people met curiosity making or listening to stories.

The history of Indian music unveils the truth that emergence of any new form never vanished the prevailing form fully. To bring about a nominal change of the prevalent form and by giving a new name, a group of musicians or a single musician declared a new form, for instance, *Khayal*. The emergence of any musical form comes out of a musician's effort and existence of higher musical forms sustained through the patronage of dominant fractions of the society. Without patronage art work and its creation can be ceased.

Hence we find two major aspects related to patronage of music. Patronage by the Aristocracy was undoubtedly associated for the survival of a particular form; at the same time court musicians were compelled to render those forms chosen by their patrons.

Therefore, the point here is quite lucid that before market economy the concept of demand and supply existed in guise in the field of music. But this concept of demand and supply could not take commercial shape for lack of modern technology and capitalist market.

4

The Dialectics of Mass Culture and the Case of Indian Music*

Music for music's sake – a principle of aesthetics could be prey to dominant social forces as societies transform through the ideology of capital. Artwork within particular set of social relationship may represent unfaithful norms to the legitimacy of the community itself and its authentic standard. A few critical thinkers employed their deep effort to understand this existing fact in the field of art and explored their own theories that are matter of academics research. Some cultural theories provide complex explanations about autonomy of artwork and class interest imposed from outside on the agents of creation.

This focus concerns culture (superstructure) rather than the base. The theories are formed on the footing of Marxist ideas and also initiated dichotomy of high culture and popular culture.

The following discourse is divided into several parts i.e., analysis of cultural theories, comparison between theories, position of music in the political economic system. The ultimate goal of discourse is to explore music industry and current trend in Indian culture.

Cultural Theories

The presence and ability of the mass to alter the nature and function of art was recognized by a number of scholars, associated with

---

* This essay first appeared in Mainstream Journal, Vol. XLIV, No. 10, February 25, 2006.

the Institute of Social Research in Frankfurt known as "The Frankfurt School". But the naming makes little sense because some scholars of the school shifted to United States in their later life. Personalities associated with the school include Theodore Adorno, Max Horkheimer, Walter Benjamin and several others.

Walter Benjamin, a respectable intellectual, an aesthete and critic of modern capitalism argued that impact of mechanical reproduction undermines the aura and the uniqueness of a single artwork. Implication of technology has reduced the quality of artwork and enabled to listen to a symphony or watch reproductions of painting any number of times. In an age of machine, collective consumption has gained its value rather than critical and intellectual judgement.

The most discussed of the scholars of Frankfurt School are T. Adorno and Max Horkheimer and their text "Dialectic of Enlightenment" (1972).

The scholars argue from an anti-positivist standpoint that the meaning of enlightenment has to be viewed critically. Enlightenment was supposed to bring freedom and intellectual thinking. But instead of bringing original meaning of Enlightenment conformity comes to effect in contemporary culture.

The scholars perceived how World War-II changed the fundamental role of culture in social production and introduced instrumental rationality.

Having devoted considerable effort the scholars viewed foundation of Nazi culture in an oppressive ideology. The cultural policy of Nazism replaced high culture with folk culture, particularly those created by German-Jews. The Nazi culture under Goebbels's propaganda ministry promoted mass culture in combination with heterogeneous cultural elements from differing Germanic ethnic groups. Adorno perceived high culture as a potential force of enlightenment and emancipation.

The scholars did not write the theory of "Culture industry" till their emigration to the United States. The theory originated out of discussion and publications in the Institute of Social

Research. Their theory is a reactionary critique of industrial capitalism and its immense control over superstructure through bureaucracy, instrumental rationality and advanced technology. The scholars traced the origin of culture industry to the latter half of the nineteenth century. They noted that till nineteenth century cultural productions depended on political and religious patronage. To achieve autonomy of artwork activities aimed to break from church and state, artistes/artists had to rely on the principles of market economy.

The concept of public sphere (repository of civil society) in Frankfurt school is a key to understand how bourgeois rose to power.

Industrialization in mid-nineteenth century awakened class conflict between pre-bourgeois class and the rising bourgeois to secure political and economic control. In this class struggle, public sphere turned into an instrument of manipulation instead of its ideological principle (freedom of public will and discussion).

To lord over the aristocracy the distinct bourgeois class focused attention to centralized control into economy at the price of snatching autonomy and implementing their private interest. This step opened the door of modern capitalism in the west.

The scholars during their project work in California were able to understand that profit-making policy of the capitalists is reflected in the investment on music movies, radio programmes, magazines and advertisement. During Princeton project Adorno wrote that transmission of live symphony is heard inferior for having improper reproduction. The ideology of production and distribution of American media is based on the intention of maximizing profit. The products of culture industry, in other words, mass cultural elements beget capitalism. Both the intellectuals adopted the term "Culture industry" as opposed to concepts like "Popular culture" or "Mass culture". Because they wanted to resist the notion that products of the culture industry emanated from the mass or from the public. Mass culture originated with rise of media like radio, television, movies, records, newspapers, magazines etc.

As mentioned earlier the term mass culture is synonymous with popular culture. Elements of mass culture are produced in combination of machine technology and products are available in the market like any other commodities. Mass culture follows the verdict of demand and supply of business cannon.

Adorno observed that the ideology of commodification went into higher music of many musicians. He noted that music of Wagner's imbibed the spirit of cultural commodification of industrial organization. To Adorno, Wagner's music employed loud sound to soften harmony. Even Beethoven's music expressed a compromise with the market to make a living.

In other words, capitalist economy reinforces to transform authentic art and size control on the autonomy of art.

In the 'Culture industry' Jazz artistes play Beethoven or Mozart's serious prices of music without adequate practice and command in playing instruments. In this way, any cultural product even of higher forms becomes synonymous with commodity.

> "The stronger the positions of culture industry, the more summarily it can deal with consumer's need producing them, controlling them, disciplining them" (Adorno, 1972: 144).

> A series of studies on popular music conducted by Adorno, one of these. "On the fetish character in music and regression of hearing" attacked standardization, commodification of musical materials in popular music.

> In light music, once the trained ear has heard the first note of the hit song, it can guess what is coming and feel flattered when it does come (Adorno, 1972: 125).

Adorno echoed Lowenthal and asserted that mass culture produces negative personalities. Contents of this culture share repetition and imitation -- an opposite to creative art.

Adorno did not appreciate every piece of high art. He advocated in particular. Avant-garde modernism. On the contrary, mass art contains trivial, poor aesthetic art elements and expression and its production is determined by business interest. In this sense, "Culture industry" as a symbol of mass deception cheats its consumers providing superficial amusement. Media contents, in "Culture industry" are determined by the capitalists and its subordinate media professionals.

The theory of "Culture industry" unravels the nature, elements of cultural product in capitalism. The theory analyses how the industry dominates artistes/artist and consumers as a pillar of capitalist mode of production.

Comparison between Theories

In contrast to theory of Adorno Antonio Gramsci (1891-1937) applied the concept "Hegemony"–the term he used to denote intellectual and moral leadership. Gramsci argued that the capitalists in alliance with the intellectual ("Organic intellectual") retained hegemony by dominating ideas and their hegemony comes to regard in capitalist society as fair and just.

Gramsci saw ordinary culture to generate alternative world-view; at the same time he was aware of the reality that popular culture with its folk and conservative religious pedestal may fail to function counter hegemony. Therefore, an allied of "Traditional intellectual" and working class might be able to subdue the authority of the capitalists. Gramsci's counter hegemony suggests a process of social change through revolutionary consciousness. Unlike Gramsci Adorno's critique to bourgeois political economy inhibits possibility of class-consciousness.

In Adorno's opinion capitalism has enslaved civil society and its industries manipulate people, obstruct collective actions. Both Adorno and Gramsci are divided up between supporter of high culture and popular culture.

Secondly, Adorno perceived masses passive, an opposition to Marxist notion of 'Revolution of the Proletariat'.

But Adorno's optimism towards high culture evokes the spirit of emancipation implicit in the meaning empowering the cultural elite.

In contrary to Adorno's view, in America and England a series of studies questioned the inherent quality of higher music like symphonies and opera. For example, Stuart Hall and Williams were concerned with rescuing creativity in popular art. Their claim departs from Adorno's view on high culture and diverts attention from higher taste to populist taste.

Moreover, empirical research into audience reception of culture shows that ordinary people may have discerning taste.

However, Adorno's theory re-establishes the fact that mass media, mass culture are intertwined with mass society.

Exploration of Music Industry

The purpose of the argument in the light of the cultural theories lies in the investigation into the culture industry in India. The following discourse will go through incorporation of music into media, commercial theatre and commercial performance. A question arises: is the economy of India is compatible with the capitalist industrialized societies?

U.R. Rao cited in the essay 'Science and technology' published in the Journal of Indian Horizon, vol. XXXXV, no. 3 and 4 July-December 1998: "India's failure to take advantage of the Industrial Revolution during the three decades of colonial rule had made it a poor industrially backward nation, totally dependent on foreign sources of all finished goods".

After independence, under the leadership of Jawaharlal Nehru India made progress in scientific and industrial research. In the dream of modern India heavy industry development received priority.

As a consequence, agricultural sector remained backward. To increase agricultural products Green Revolution in 1960s resulted in a vast area under cultivation.

During 1970-80 inflation as well as oil price hike compelled India to go for loan from the IMF.

Moreover, from mid-eighties the country adopted the policy of liberalizing the economy. As a result, industrial growth rate and production in agriculture increased.

Again in 1990 India faced crisis due to Gulf war.

But since 1991 economic growth rate witnessed height on account of developments on industry, trade, finance and exchange rate.

Even if the last few years' growth rate has been showing seven per cent, still excessive population, illiteracy rate, living below poverty line indicate the country belongs to developing nations.

What is evident is that India has had the burden of colonial imperialism.

In pre-independence era radio stations opened in Bombay, Calcutta, Madras, Dacca and some other places have been patron of classical music, since 1920s.

Alongside a business class named organizers, fund collectors as well as well-wishers of funding companies used to advertise in the same souvenir, brochure of annual, bi-annual music conference held for musicians.

This was the beginning of music to come closer to the masses as *durbars* and court patronage broke.

As a matter of fact, media technology such as Press, Radio, TV, Gramophone Company was adopted in India via colonial rule.

The study of Gerry Farell focuses attention on business interest of Gramophone Company as well as benefaction of mass musical culture. By the twentieth century due to political and social change brought by British Raj, new patrons of the market-places replaced an older form of musical patronage. The adaptation of modernization process alongside emergence of urban business class, followed by commercial interest, made significant impact in the field of music. A number of musicians agreed to record only three and a half minutes *Khayal* and *Thumri* with the response to the market.

Although in reproduction laws of Gramophone Company classical music dominated but regional popular songs (*Bangla Adhunic Gana)* and folk songs also incorporated.

Cinema to be carrier of popular entertainment came in India almost at the same time as in other film producing countries. Film songs with its simple tune and rhythm attracted masses. Film songs in a form of industrial manufactured goods are available in the market; its consumption can be compared to any other commodities associated with advertising. Until the mid-nineties popular music in India mostly covered filmy music. But the coming of the two music video channels, namely MTV and [V] brought about a sea change in the prevailing entertainment business.

Popular singer Alisha's 'Made in India', Daler Mehendi's *Bolo Tara Ra* (*Bhangra*) sold respectively 2.2 million and 1.5 million copies. These boosts in popular music clearly indicate commercial success, but the questions of cultivated audiences exclude in reception of such songs.

MTV (India) and channel [V] India promote amateurs to present Remixes, Indi-Pop, in the manner of western Pop, Rock, Reggae, Hip-hop, R & B. Those who have trained ear may feel like the production of *swara* (note) has low intensity and lower magnitude; these factors have much importance in case of western popular forms i.e., Hard rock, Hip-hop, Jazz and R & B. Therefore, demand of these songs persists in Inland not in the world music. At times video transmission of Punjabi folk songs represent dresses and disco dance of the western popular singers.

Failing to sing according to conventional style, sometimes one may listen to a *chotta khayal's* composition presented with the aid of Drumbeat instead of *Tabla* and *Byaa* and a few other western instruments by means of distorted *Tala* (time).

Experimental fusion music videos act to confuse musically literate audiences to classify what form of music it is? For Adorno, popular songs assist unhealthy mental state and its hearing produces regression. Here, I agree with Adorno on the point that contemporary popular songs do not engender delight.

Contemporary video music wherein scanty musical properties combined with erotic behaviour and dance represent nightclubs, bar. Therefore, bluntly speaking music video sell basically erotic behavior and fun. Here, role of music is mediated by trade law.

> K.J. Kumar writes in his book, Mass Communication in India thus:... Audio cassettes, which are cheaper, continue to dominate the Indian market of a hundred million consumers. CD players have to be imported at inflated prices and thus far beyond the reach of these consumers. Almost every major international player in the global music business

has a presence in India. These include EMI, Virgin Records, Sony Music Entertainment, Warner Bros., Polygram, BMG-crescando, CBS Records, Gramco and others.

The Gramophone Company in India popularly known as gramco or HMV since its arrival in 1907 to till date has been acting as a unit of 'culture industry' having inspired the capitalists for the expansion of music industry within. Therefore, what is apparent, a New World of culture already in existence in India.

Current Trends

From philosophical standpoint music is the most abstract form of art, which represents life process of a society. To Adorno, higher music conveys messages of salvation–an approach of hermeneutics, which Adorno wanted to highlight.

Although Adorno condemned mass music but in reality many Pop and Rock stars in the west incorporated social consciousness in lyrics and some of their songs composed to protest against racism, war, in favour of nature conservation.

On the contrary, contemporary popular songs in India basically represent the aspect of human life i.e., sensuality. Moreover, newly created popular songs encounter crisis of 'Cultural Identity' for lack of institutional base. In such an era, where media patronize amateurs what could be the position of classical music?

Answer can be given one dimensionally–living in contradiction with the high/popular binary of capitalist culture. Now-a-days one can observe a set of compromising artistes as well as the purists. Third category includes basically concert-giving artistes whose activities are inspired by the practice of carrying coal to the new organizers.

The purists even in an era of commerce do not embrace contemporary practices, not even have compromised due to their responsibility to subjective laws of music. They rather select defeat to the objective cannons in the field. At times, they express nostalgia towards court patronage and thus become alienated into the dictate of the market and demand of musically ignorant masses.

The most striking of the prevailing situations in the world of music is that the concept of *Gharana* is on the brink of fall.

Gharanas that are not progressive enough from aesthetic logic but sustain through assimilation till today.

Particularly, popular vocalists of *Benaras Gharana* have fused features of *Kirana Gharana, Samchaurasi Gharana;* nonetheless they refuse to admit how much they owe to those *Gharanas*.

Were Adorno alive and he visited India would have reshaped the conception of "Mass deception".

Rapid growth of entertainment by TV channels apart from MTV and channel [V] has drawn attention of the youth and fun loving social classes. Transmission of dance music enjoys great popularity and contributes to influence outlook of the young, businessmen and the elite of some fraction in Indian society. Nightclubs and five star hotels have its arrangement of Western popular dance to meet demand.

The shift announces accelerated rise of commercial media and its texts signal a wider reception of mass culture and market economics.

Therefore, what is observed is that the ideology of consumer capitalism has already entered into society partially; at the same time traditional values, institution and unequal life standard are inseparable from social system.

Central to Adorno's argument I also perceive classical music in India and its bearers are being challenged owing to the impact of newly popular forms.

Over the decades, nationally and centrally controlled media board went to the private sectors.

Studios for making video music, audio music; cassettes and CD, releasing companies all together have opened unobstructed choices of the buyers. Cassettes and CDs of classical music receive least attention, most of the reproduction of classical music covers old masters and music of a few commercially successful artistes. Mass scale production of popular songs. in contrast, demarcated production of classical music. It reveals the triumph of mass musical culture and its market value.

In conclusion, work of art influenced by business motif cause to produce inferior creations. In this sense, art represents contradictions; domination in societies, notwithstanding, art music chooses its existence in the dialectic between aesthetic logic and the social classes who control the base.

5

Class Struggle in the Field of Cultural Production

This chapter attempts to find struggles among agents of music in the light of Pierre Bourdieu's Theory.

Pierre Bourdieu was a professor and an intellectual of cultural theory. His thinking owes to Marx's materialism and Weber's thesis of differentiation.

Bourdieu adopts critical attitude to implicate statistical method to grasp social world. He emphasized that real world cannot be apprehended through experiment report collected from laboratory wherein social behavior is observed in controlled situation.

He views that human actions are outcome of objectively adjusted social conditions in which it is constituted within a constraining social world.

P. Bourdieu's theory of field and *habitus* voice structuralism to grasp French literary field, fine art and to some extent music from subjective and objective principles wherein the role played by the active social agents becomes minimized or revolutionary. In the cultural field Bourdieu noticed that impressionist Manet refused institutional canons of aesthetic value and led his activities in opposition of the belief 'art for art's sake'. This initiated breakdown of institutional conventional forms and plurality paved its way in the field of painting instead of single legitimized authority. After Manet a new group of artists came in the field of painting who take little care for a single source of legitimacy.

The notion of field is a dynamic process in the struggle of position taking and distribution of available position by different agents to achieve legitimacy. Internal logic of an artistic field in particular high culture could be shaken by the objective logic due to new circumstances in production, consumption and circulation.

It is merely an effort to use Bourdieu's model to apprehend Indian music in relation to objective structures in the network of production and distribution, external changes exerted on internal logic of the field (universe).

Field as Force Field

Earlier, *gharanedar* musicians enjoyed greatest privilege of being court musicians. But political situation in pre-independence India caused unavoidable situation due to colonial rule and impact of modernity.

For India, music in institutions deserves greater value on account that apart from practical teaching musicology remains side by side. As a consequence, the frontier of research expanded.

Classical music was replaced (as the monopoly of *gharanedar* musicians) by involvement of non-*gharanedar* showed new vista in the field.

The changing social role of the artiste in modern time clearly reveals complexities. Reception in present day is wider than aristocratic patronage both for India and the West. Art has been conceived as an expression of society; in this sense my point of argument is music represents society symbolically to exemplify, life situations of artistes in modern era is more critical particularly who deal with higher form of art. Artistic production has to find out exchange value at present scenario. Today artiste's work depends on the satisfaction of buyers (consumers for instance, organizers, audiences, Record Company). The whole artistic network has put on the feature of market economy. Art does not any more serve elitist class interest alone. Cultural movement is one of these reasons.

In musical production the most disputed issue is observed i.e. existence of dualism in teaching method, on the one hand traditional *Guru-Shishya* method on the other hand, institutionalized music teaching accompanied with degrees, and diploma. Mushrooming music schools are contributing to music education. This category of teaching method is not compatible with the status of traditional *guru-shishya parampara. Guru-Shishya Parampara* can be viewed almost autonomous and indifferent to any social change but during employment in institution degree holders predominate in universities and free lance artistes are deprived for not having institutional degree. Cultural capital in the form of degree is considered as artistic prestiges (degrees can be converted to economic capital) conversely, concert, conferences are dominated by mostly free-lance artistes.

In India, free-lance artistes considerably contribute to the production by imparting their applied knowledge to disciples wherein training takes place at their residence. At times some *gurus* visit disciples' residence if he/she is paid high fees. *Guru-Shishya Parampara* is a traditional oral teaching method based on basic memory, ability to give practical performance, (although lyrics or *bandishes*, some theories remain written by hand) practical demonstration, and listening dominate at large. Unlike western music system it's dependency lies in notation much.

The matter to ponder is that status of freelance artistes at concurrent cultural situation displays a downward economic stature due to rapid growth of academies, music colleges and music as a major subject in universities. It will not be unjustified to call institutions as patron of music. Moreover the members of these institutions keep contact with government, corporate finally influencing the field. Music institutions also contribute to raise interest in music among the masses.

But it does not sound good over decades that institutions failed to produce quality artistes although it contributes a lot to produce seminar, books, research work, academic, music executives etc. One of the reasons is that a in-depth study is ignored here, therefore, free-lancers hold institutions for producing inferior performers and it is evident that *gharanedar* artistes from past to present day have been capable of producing real performers. It is an irony of the institutions that quality artistes never grow in institutions. At the same time institutions and its personnel have no confidence in free-lance artiste whether they can furnish lecture-cum-demonstration. A few good performers as well as musical academics excel in writing an article, essay on music in modern era.

As a matter of fact, both the prevailing systems contribute to construct structure of the field, despite internal conflicts.

Bourdieu viewed artistic field as a force field. The base of force comes out of possession of certain type of cultural capital, i.e. cultural taste, degrees, competent performance, ability to furnish lecture-cum-demonstration.

To Bourdieu cultural capital takes time to attain and it is incorporated in our sense of the self. One of the features is transposability. Cultural capital works in a wider social structure. Bourdieu analysed that in the second half of the nineteenth century French cultural field struggled over the problem of art and money, pure and commercial art. This struggle aimed at two basic purposes i.e. power struggle of the dominant group and the legitimacy over cultural products.

However, apart from internal logic inherent in the structure, external determinants also function as force in the field. The point deserves to mention here is that Karl Marx considered economic capital as marker of class distinction while for Bourdieu, it is the cultural capital.

External determinism came into prominence with the emergence of market economy resulting patrons of the market i.e., media industry traders and the mass audience. As a consequence, emergence of middlemen (organizers) and intermediary group, media professionals and marketers also appeared to work for music to take it to every doorstep.

From medieval period to modern era symbolic capital (honour to be court musician) shows an eye catching change in commercial era in respect to subordination of music to economic capital of the capitalist and purchasing ability of musical products by mass audience.

Musical academics in institutions undoubtedly enjoy certainty of economic capital but the life situation of *gharanedar* musicians is a matter of bemoan. Their earnings basically come from private tuitions; to some extent giving sporadic concert even at privately organized social parties. While some performing artistes have chosen foreign land for patronage because many non-resident Indians arrange concert for them and at times artistes have privilege as music trainers. In one sense, it makes little difference between working class and the artistes. Modernization process in India under British imperialism turned the artiste's position upside down as it was in olden days. New situation taught *gharanedar* musicians to impart music outside the lineage who belonged to educated middle class. This new class in the universe accelerated the growth of music in institutions. S.M. Tagore, V.N. Bhatakhande and V.D. Paluskar the three great personalities encouraged learning of musicology alongside practical training.

Secondly, some artistes in post-independence era paid much attention to interest of economic profitability and heterogeneous audiences. Consequently new set of artistes as well as new audience weakened the symbolic power (prestige) of *gharanedar* musicians to some extent. Symbolic power is a sign of those past days when many *gharanedar* musicians enjoyed the status of being court musicians. Any change in social structures in a given moment of history considerably effect the subjective and objective relation between creators and consumers. In other words unpredictability of the artistic field may introduce new conditions to keep up or adjust with the field. It ultimately influences the structure of the artistic field.

Thirdly, sponsored concerts are situate between objective set of social relations of product promotion in the name of patronage of art music. Concert symbolizes actually group behavior. Agents of concert are namely, organizer, artiste, percussionist, secretary, acoustic mechanics or engineers, stage makers, announcer and also media professionals. One agent of concerts i.e. fund collectors whose real name is organizers or middleman or so called promoters are actually the product of expansion of music trade.

This class can be termed gatekeepers who live in between mediation to business class and the artistes. The positions of organizers lie in assuring musical production in keeping with business interest and gratifying of the varied taste of masses.

P. Bourdieu called this specific principle bourgeoisie taste as well as the taste of the mass audience.

Structure of Cultural Field

P. Bourdieu noted two fundamental oppositions in the structure of cultural field i.e., field of restricted production and the field of large-scale production. The former produces those artworks which stranded on the principle of art for art's sake, the latter value commercial cannon at the cost of producing artwork similarly any other commodities in the market.

In the division of labour of cultural production, restricted field of production objectively designed for the same community (artistes) conversely large-scale production intends to supply for public demand. Field of cultural production is a universe of belief in this light. According to Bourdieu in French society art critic emerged to make solidarity between the artists and the field, Bourdieu says, review acts to transform the structure of the field through redefining the creation. In contrast, in the realm of Indian music criticism did not gain confidence in artistic community for lack of professionalism and objective attitude. Most music critics in India conceive criticism merely the fault of performers with a view to establish himself/herself as somebody very important in the circle of music. Another set of critics merely write favourable criticism to highlight their chosen artistes. Speaking rather bluntly, constructive music criticism is rarely found in newspaper, journal by which some artistes can mould, reshape their style.

Duly negative criticism towards upcoming artistes may discourage the newcomers to stop cultural practices in many cases. On the other hand positive appreciation which may come out of a good communication between the artiste and critic is able to provide special attention, position in the field. In fact music criticism in India still waiting for maturity. Critics of India after any concert do not project artiste's view about choice of *raga* or his/her style of presentation. An upcoming artist is unaware of what review he/she is going to receive from the critic. In many cases even competent artistes do not find fare criticism. Therefore, this unpredictable condition of music review has caused much dissatisfaction in the community of artistes. After all critics' judgement should be viewed personal opinion not scientific one. Sometimes the gap between critic's understanding and the way creator makes meaning reveal a large difference in the field. Actually, critics also are not above rules. Critics have been given position in press and he justifies that he/she has the right to write. Therefore, in the field of art world critic can be viewed also a dominant class under some conditions he/she should be objective in analysis of artworks. If not, any artiste's accusation of unfair writing even can overthrow the post. Hence, both the artistes and the critics are agents of counter domination in artistic field.

Bourdieu credits French educational system since it is conducive to develop taste for high art. The French society of his time was placing a greater value on high culture with a view to confirm their status. Competition among various institutions for cultural consecration to re-produce producers at the same time to make consumers able to receive their cultural goods lead a competition and also raise the point of hierarchy. Bourdieu noted that the hierarchy of high art and popular art symbolize that society is differentiated. All modern societies including India also belong to class bound societies.

In a social system, the works of art and its agents (i.e. producer) encounter differing authority of legitimacy. Apart from educational system there are other authorities of legitimization, either semi-institutional or collective production unit like radio, TV, magazine and personnel associated with such institution and unit.

In India, AIR gradation board and organization of musicians (music societies in a diffused manner), publicists etc. are authorities, but the less expressive and most acceptable legitimacy comes from the competent artistes of the community itself. In other words established artistes and their comment on other artistes even in informal conversation heard by anybody are considered seriously.

All relations among agents and institution of consecration or diffusion are intertwined by the structure of the field. To Bourdieu, *habitus* contributes to form the subjective aspiration (motivation) to occupy position. The history of field reveals the struggle between the established and the young challengers i.e., consecrated avant-garde and avant-garde.

Coming to India hereditary *Kirana Gharana* vocalist Amir Khan named his style *Indore Gharana* and Amjad Ali Khan (*Sarodist*) of *Seniya Gharana* renamed his *Gharana Seniya Bangash Gharana*. In fact, individual interest and motivated struggles benefited particular *gharana* but it could not generate artistic revolution in India as it happened in European art partially.

These changes in Indian music can be described as dominant/ dominated clash; underlying goals is to secure individual position in the field, not collective one. But these shifts ensure displacement in the field in relation to position occupied by the dominant one.

However in Bourdieu's French society, one agent of cultural production did not appear named *Chamcha*.

Chamcha

Chamcha is a generic name to describe an agent who is critical to other artistes but uncritical to artists/artistes he/she prefers. Here lies the difference between a *Chamcha* and critic, One is judgemental and the other is not judgemental.

A *chamcha* could be a learner, kinsman of a particular *gharana* or member of an institute. *Chamcha's* subjective aspiration (motivation) could lead to construct objective probabilities i.e., to have an access in the field or simply to be liked.

Chamcha has great potential to act like an unofficial publicist to preach about his/her chosen artistes. In fact *Chamcha's* appreciation about his chosen artistes is given some value in the field. If *Chamcha's* selected artistes receive chance to perform in conference after performance loud claps produced by *Chamcha's* can draw easy attention of the whole gathering. *Chamcha's* ideology is based on forming lobby. Thus the role played by *Chamcha* largely contribute an unequal distribution of programme. *Chamcha* is also an informant to raise awareness about what other artistes' groups are doing. In this way *Chamcha* also plays a role in cultural production.

In the struggle for relative legitimacy between position and position taking *habitus* acts as mediator.

Habitus

Bourdieu's concept of *habitus* is somewhat an elusive term. He refers it the systems of durable, transposable dispositions and structures.

Bourdieu argues that in the field of strategy trajectory followed by agents result from unconscious disposition of practice. In another space Bourdieu says that *habitus* originates from cognition achieved in the past and motivation at present situation that directs to furnish expected target at any given moment. *Habitus* is the universalizing mediation, which causes an individual's practice.

Habitus ranges from agents to group or class *habitus*. But Bourdieu was lucid in his apprehension that every member of the same class might not have same experience and disposition. For instance, offspring of Amjad Ali Khan (*Sarodist*) and Ravi Shankar (*Sitarist*) display *habitus* towards popular culture as well as high culture. Although musically novice, standard of their performance raise question but strategy and trajectory they adopt reveal that they are encashing symbolic capital (prestige, established artistes) of their father to get entry in the field. Therefore, what is evident is that field of cultural production is a space of contention for position taking or possible space among varying creative agents culminating dynamic shift in the structure of the universe.

To Bourdieu, *habitus* is also unequally distributed among agents.

People of subordinate position are not equipped with *habitus* to go for life improvement actions. Bourdieu suggests that family standard of education plays a role in the differential allocation of *habitus*. So *habitus* causes inequality in social system.

Criticism

As every theory has limitations so does Bourdieu's theory. Bourdieu's one dimensionally attributes family and institution to develop *habitus*. In fact, concomitant societies, media contents contribute a lot to develop taste for popular culture.

In the analysis of Bourdieu's *habitus* Alan Swingwood comments that his theory of *habitus* suggests a limited notion of agents or the self and not a reflexive social self whose social and cultural identity arises out of complex interaction with others. *Habitus* both organizes practices and allows for the perception of practices.

Fluctuation may occur in *habitus* durability to cope with life situation. For instance, many *gharanedars* now-a-days teach *Ghazal* alongside pure forms of classical music in demand of their disciples. This practice in fact is unfavourable to their *habitus* rather it is a means of livelihood merely. Therefore, we notice that in some cases instead of durability forceful transfiguration takes place in individual *habitus* to make space for monetary gain.

Field

Bourdieu's field is a site between field, sub-field and active agents within, over high and popular culture, between legitimacy over established order to emerging new artistic valuation, between dominant and dominated, all these struggles ultimately being undertaken to gain economic capital.

In Indian musical parlance dispute is observed between institutional teaching method and the traditional oral system, free-lancers and the academics. In this struggle, free-lancers (not necessarily all) are more competitive to avail of sponsored concerts, which ensure economic capital as well as publicity. In this game instrumentalists are ahead.

Bourdieu's theory of field does not focus much about reception of cultural products. Reception assists to evolution of a particular artistic genre, through ceaseless production and its absence can cause stagnation in specific genre. (See chapter 3)

Secondly, Bourdieu's field is a site of power structure over scarce resources. But it leaves the question unresolved about introvert artistes who are not very fond of involving themselves in power structure, publicity or achieving symbolic status (award, honour). For example, many artistes in the history of Indian music refused State offered title *Padma Bhusan and the like on the accusation of untimely state recognition though they deserved award long ago.*

Whatever the limitations are, Bourdieu's model to understand different cultural practices through *habitus* and the concept of field provide a comprehensible account to define artistic field, agent's activities and power structure of class bound societies.

6

Mechanization and Culture

A Critical Analysis

The discourse in this chapter will unfold why India could not head for timely development toward capitalism. Secondly the chapter is an effort to investigate link between music and technological assistance wherein my objective is to explore both positive and negative factors of music in association with technology.

Creation in association with technology is able to transform uniqueness of artwork was admitted by W. Benjamin an intellectual of Frankfurt school. A single piece of novel, musical form can turn into enormous novels, cassettes, and CDs with the combined effort of technicians and their technical operation of machines. In simple words, these industrial cultural products of creative activities are reproduction of machine age. But prior to invention of electronic media there persisted technology of instrument making, for instance, *Sitar, Sarod, Tanpura*, Harmonium, Piano etc., adduced to implication of technical knowledge.

In fact modern technology is the outcome of technological invention followed by industrialization. The key to understand the concept of machine age is industrialization.

Under the process of capitalist economic and socio-system people of these societies profusely experienced positive-negative effects caused by the setback. Interestingly when Western Europe shifted to industrial revolution, India remained behind.

Two contradictory theories are burning issues in sociology concerning why these societies could make way to capitalism. Two famous classical German sociologists Weber and Marx wrote their theories from two different dimensions. Max Weber's theory emphasizes on ideas and belief system; on the other hand, Karl Marx's theory on forces of production and material possession. According to Karl Marx, bourgeois revolution, scientific development in technology, appearance of manufacture and its application in material production are the determining factors in the formation of industrial capitalism.

Karl Marx and Engles described the nature of capitalist productive force in the Manifesto of the communist party in this manner.

Subjection of nature's forces to man, machinery, application of chemistry to industry and agriculture, steam navigation, railways, electric telegraphs, clearing of whole continents for cultivation, canalization of rivers, whole populations conjured out the ground.

In contrast, in the Protestant Ethic and the spirit of capitalism Weber attempted to identify how religious beliefs and self-interests had influenced economic behavior. Weber held that Calvinism was a significant force in the formation of capitalism.

To Calvin self-discipline is the nerve of religion. Hence self-denial became a virtue among many. Believers of Calvinism denied present desires for future rewards e.g. staying away from gambling, drinking and luxuries. According to M. Weber many early Protestants believed in hard work as a moral and religious duty. The Protestants increasingly emphasized on capitalist enterprise.

Most of their profits were available for investment. Calvin taught that everyone is to glorify God and to work for the creation of a divine kingdom on earth. Calvin emphasized that the proper aim of humanity is not personal salvation. There was nothing evil about investing or lending money at moderate interest.

Weber's thesis explained that religious doctrine of John Calvin (Geneva) led to Puritan to go into business and making money. The concept of predestination by Calvin was based on the theme that nobody knows if one was destined for heaven or hell. But there is only one escape – that is hard work, at the same time good work. The Puritan being motivated by Calvinism started to act hard to flourish business and production with the ideology of market economy. This rationality of belief system led to the accumulation of wealth and transforming society to modern capitalism.

In the interpretation of Protestantism Randall Collins writes:

That Weber saw religion as having a major effect in producing modern capitalism... Across Europe as a whole, there was a new openness of religious thought. This in itself created something of a mood of anxiety. It was a highly religious age, in which the church was present everywhere in everyday life, and going to sermons was even used as a source of entertainment (in the absence of much else). The afterlife, salvation or damnation, heaven or hell, were constantly drummed into people's ears. Hence the question of how to achieve salvation was an important one, especially because the orthodox view was made unsure by competing conceptions. This religious tension, Weber felt, was an important source of social motivation, as it made people strongly concerned to do whatever was necessary to save themselves.

In this situation, the most challenging theological position was that taken by the Calvinists. The doctrine was formulated by John Calvin in Geneva, but it spread across Europe especially in the Presbyterian Church, which became politically important in Scotland, and in the revolutionary movement in England. The major point of Calvin's doctrine was predestination. Since God is all powerful and all knowing, there is nothing that He cannot do or know. God knows the entire past and the entire future, and by His power He has ordained everything that is to be. This implies that everything that everyone does is already predetermined.

Naturally this caused a lot of anxiety among people for whom the tortures of hell were a vividly accepted reality. It did not help matters that Calvin declared, we are all sinners, and hence all deserved to go to hell. Only the divine grace of God left a narrow escape route. God had preordained that some few, the so-called elect, had been chosen to be saved. It did not happen through anyone's actions or will; one could not buy one's way into heaven, by saying prayers, going to mass... Sociologically speaking, Calvin's... effort to negate all of the tactics of the Catholic Church he was rebelling against. But the effect was that people believed only the sheer mercy of God could save anyone from hell.

The result of this religious doctrine, then, was to produce anxiety and a strong motivation to discipline one's life in every respect. The doctrine of predestination ended up producing hard work; one's whole life became a religious effort. The irony of this situation is that the Puritans became rich. Their business flourished; they became leading citizens. Capitalism grew, but Puritanism began to fade away. The Protestant ethic, precisely because of its effects in transforming the world eventually undermined itself.

Here we find a fundamental difference between Karl Marx's and Weber's standpoint about social change. Marx's viewed social change from materialistic understanding while Max Weber saw social change in terms of religious motivation.

Max Weber, at the same time, commented that India having had the favourable conditions to step to capitalism but failed as Europe had already marched for capitalism. First of all Weber argued that traditional caste system is one of the reasons why India lagged behind. He blamed the nature of caste system for being hereditary that hindered to social mobility. In Weber's opinion, European guilds were not hereditary. Secondly, Weber said that western cities became an independent unit, based on a coalition of its leading members.

In other words, European cities were coalition of guilds. But in India the guilds could not take form into coalition. Because of Hindu religion and its caste based hierarchy, the business class never enjoyed much social status. That is why wealthy merchants could not turn their resources into political power.

Max Weber's theory about the emergence of capitalism in the Western Europe and India's backwardness despite the existence of material infrastructure of capitalism is highly debatable. Firstly, Weber overemphasized the ethics of Protestantism rather not focusing on the industrial revolution as the key to social transformation.

English historian R.H. Tawney wrote:

> It was this practical basis of urban industry and commercial enterprise that the structure of Calvinist social ethics erected. (Tawney, 1938, p.117)

According to sociologist Kautsky where commerce and early forms of industrialization already established the ethics of Calvinism was accepted by the business class to legitimate their position and activities.

Secondly, India had constraints imposed by British colonialism. It is a quest if Indian business class received real market price having supplied raw materials in England. Such important points are missing in Weber's interpretation.

Professor A.K. Nazmul Karim wrote, in the seventeenth and eighteenth century, we find conditions similar to those of Europe when capitalism was making its first headway and financiers were supplying the needs of waging wars as well as for running the day-to-day administration. (Karim, 1976, p. 22)

Quoting M.N. Roy, Nazmul Karim had written, he was the first to appreciate that even before British rule, Indian society had undergone a vital change in the economic arena which created possibilities for its transformation into a capitalist society... The barter economy was being replaced by a money economy and we find that the Mughal treasury was minting more and more cash. The increase in international trade in the later period the huge influx of gold and silver which must had led to brisk activity in business and production. (ibid, 1976, pp. 86-89)

The British East India Company came in India with free trade colonialism and motivation to intensify domination in India after the victory in 1857 at the battle of Plassey. Professor N.K. Karim commented that the Indian trading class who could not capture political power due to peculiarity of Indian society, but they helped the British merchant capitalist in the expansion of their trade, internal troubles; internecine wars between the rival principalities paved the path for English merchant class to capture India politically.

The colonial rule established money economy, new type of state policy, a new educational system; British rule introduced into India social as well as technological inventions. (Bottomore, 1986, p. 304). British imperialism also brought with them media industry in India.

In 1907 Gramophone Company first came into India with a commercial interest. Indian broadcasting company was opened in 1927, a private company after the financial success of European broadcasting. Lionel Fielden became India's first controller of Broadcasting. The bottom line is under the aegis of colonial power, India headed for Industrialization. Industrialization had considerable impact on Indian society.

During the pre-British period the urban commercial classes satisfied to play a role subordinate to the courts and noblemen, the soldiers, officials, priests and pilgrims, who collectively constituted the "Consumer Class" and who in the possession of the towns but under the British rule, all production, rural or urban, agricultural or industrial, became production for the market. As a result the internal markets expanded and the class of traders engaged in internal trade grew in numbers. It was during the British rule that India became linked more intimately and extensively with the world market. The class of merchants who now traded with foreign countries steadily increased in importance. (ibid, 1976, p.102).

Indian society in the face of transition and to become modernized its second phase of industrialization started during 1950s to 1960s under the leadership of Jawaharlal Nehru. In 1959 Delhi Television Centre was installed.

Having collected data from V.C. Khare's paper Keval J. Kumar wrote thus: cable networks across the country have installed Satellite Dishes to pick up the television channels of STAR-TV and Doordarshan and to-retransmit them via cable to around 2,00,000 cable networks in the country.

Kumar added more information from the reporting of Times of India- SITI cable (of the ZEE TV Network) and INCABLENET (of the Hinduja Group) are the two largest consortia in the cable business and the majority of cable operators have joined one or the other group so as to keep up with the competition. In Bombay alone, INCABLENET has 6,00,000 and SITI Cable 4,00,000 cable connections under their control out of a total of 12,00,000 connections. Small time cable operators control a mere 2,00,000 connections. (Kumar, 2002, p. 222).

It is assumed by many that cultural products in association with technology have increased the quality and quantity of cultural products. Media industries all over the world function to broadcast various recorded or live programmes on Sports, Fine Arts, Music, News, Movies, Soap Opera, Documentary etc. These programmes have direct, indirect influence on individuals to societies as a whole. Novel technological invention and its use in music increase the size of the audiences as well as various producers. Video music in 1970s in the west associated with music, fashion, narrative, fascinated huge public than ever before. Here making video music is a profitable business. It has effected listening of radio music programmes, cassette, long play, audios record etc. It is an evidence of quantitative expansion of music production as well as consumption. Reproducibility with the aid of corporate investment expanded the market of popular music. In this present day digital reproduction using personal computer has caused loss in quality but reproduction has blurred distinction between the original and reproduction to the consumers.

Various forms of intervention in cultural products from pre-industrial to industrial social stage (capitalism) and relations of production of these societies caused concern for the intellectuals of western European countries. All the intellectuals (Frankfurt School) have one thing in common that they perceived capitalist mode of production antithesis to pure cultural creation. Moreover, commercial interest underlying any creative activities has raised the ideological concern in relation to quality of artwork among Western Marxist or left wing intellectuals.

Even the most perfect reproduction of a work of art is lacking in one element. Its presence in time and space, its unique existence at the place where it happens to be... Technical reproduction can put the copy of the original into situation which would be out of reach for the original itself. Above all, it enables the original to meet the beholder halfway, be it in the form of a photograph or a phonograph record. The cathedral leaves its locale to be received in the studio of a lover of art; the choral production, performed in an auditorium or in the open air, resounds in the drawing room. (Benjamin, 1970, pp. 222-23)

Walter Benjamin became critical to the application of technology on artwork. 'The work of art in the age of mechanical reproduction' this Essay of Benjamin provides basically aesthetic explanation of music and fine art. He mentioned some techniques such as printing, photography, film, recording systems that are manufacturing mass level reproduction. Reproductions make artwork more accessible. An admirer of painting can view a print any time or a listener of music can play his/her chosen music sitting, standing anywhere. He advocated artwork of pre-industrial societies because those artworks revealed uniqueness and authenticity. But artwork in association with technology has become routinised and standardized. He analyzed when a piece of master art is displayed in art gallery; it becomes harder to organize the response of the masses. He says that aesthetic power of traditional artwork is interrelated with the combination of uniqueness, authenticity and authority. By mechanical reproduction W. Benjamin means large-scale replication of cultural artifact by the means of machineries. He says that replica is a source of mass consumption such as watching movie in a cinema hall. He writes "the public is an examiner, but an absent-minded one".

What W. Benjamin wanted to convey is that image of artwork takes different shape after reproduction. Secondly, higher art is also consumed by the masses; it is no more an elitist consumption.

In the light of Benjamin's theory, a discourse of Indian classical music will uncover that scholars of Indian music are also concerned about the effect of electronic media in music.

In the opinion of Dr. Leela Omchery:

The natural musical abilities have been replaced by the electronically supplied resources, to which the whole art world is a slave. There is hardly any musical expression without electronic aids.... A great performance becomes a miserable experience through a defective soundboard mechanism and vice-versa. An audition or a recording at the studios, everything can be enhanced or spoiled. The system being highly sensitive, not only erratic recording, but also transferred or out of place emphasis also may affect the effect of recital. This can be often experienced while listening or viewing some of the recording of the AIR, TV etc. The faulty sitting arrangement of the leading artiste and his accompanists and wrong focus on the musical production, often mar a good recital.... So, instead of becoming a useful and imaginative piece of audio art, a recorded item often tends to be mechanical, clumsy and boring. (Vageshwari, Vol. VII, 1995, pp. 45-46)

Two contrast views are written by Dr. Shanno Khurana thus:

Pre-recorded music in the way of audio cassettes, compact discs, long playing records, spools, is another wonder of this age. When music was not recorded and the performance was unique, the splendid exquisite flow of notes and nuances though lent exuberance colour, at that particular moment gave pleasure to the performer and the listener, but then was lost, because, there was no gadget to capture these for all times. Now through electronic media we have this faculty. Pre-recorded cassettes, CDs, LPs, records, spools of rare music are there for the asking .... Callousness, disinterest in the production, using bad quality or used tapes, taking musicians for granted, discourtesy or non-maintenance of musical instruments are all deterrent to producing good music. (ibid, pp. 28-29)

The bottom line is lack of professionalism in using electronic devices in music reproduction in India concerns the scholars. Expert sound engineers are able to enhance bad voice a good voice, inferior tonal quality of some instrumentalists could be reproduced better than original one.

Singh Bandhu prominent scholars of Indian Music has presented beneficiary role of technology –

> In the realm of arts too, technology has played its useful role and influenced it both in content and form. Computerized painting, which was scoffed, has recently been appreciated by some of the modern artist ... synthesizer, the computer based instrument, works as one-man orchestra to produce a variety of musical sounds and rhythms by the press of a button. Microphone increases the volume of human voice to reach a large gathering assembled in a big hall or open space. Microphone helps in the execution of finer elements and nuances such as *Murkis, Khatkas* and *Zarabs* more effectively when rendered in a natural voice. (ibid, p. 32)

The scholars have pointed out the positive aspects of technology. Having attended many concerts I have experienced that in most cases before the concert stage rehearsal is ignored in cultural programmes. Moreover sound engineers, sound operators (not all of them) do not have proper aesthetic knowledge the way voice or instrumental sound should be reproduced. The lack of knowledge at time spoils even a good performance by creating irritation in hearing.

Pulak Barua a Sound Engineer of Promix recording Studio comments thus:

> Digital recording has reduced duration of recording. At times digital recording intentionally spoils natural voice or instrumental sound to adjust with market principal. Due to the technique of editing sound engineers can heighten weak performance of both vocal and instrumental form. In the digital recording system there is option of resetting out of tune performance to tuneful singing to some extent. But after reproduction mass audiences cannot find what actually was the real singing. Digital recording is capable of giving new tone even bad vocals.

What is evident is that both application of mechanical devices and music reproduced through machines create positive and negative effects. Whatever the consequences are, the fact is that India borrowed modern communication technology to share with development process.

Of audio-visual media programmes in India Doordarshan and ZEE TV network are worth mentioning. At the beginning Doordarshan programme strenuously captivated viewers of India. Commercialization of Doordarshan is considerably rising today despite authorities from music world raise dissatisfaction very often on account of Doordarshan spare a little time on classical music programmes. ZEE TV is basically entertainment network meaning – programmes are based on mainly with elements of mass culture with a view to gratify the public and the promoter of mass/ popular culture.

Although communication has reduced the world through globalization process but for many people obscured and distorted message conveyed by the media is misleading. Gabriele Dietrich pointed out a very crucial aspect about the impact of communication thus:

> ... The industrialization of communication has contributed to large-scale de-skilling in traditional arts like music, dance, drama, recitations, debate, poetry etc. The media also set a stereotyped standard of performance in these arts which often stifle initiative and originality. ... The habit of consuming TV develops in total alienation from the seasons of the year, the events of the life cycle, the actual working and living condition of the people.

Whatever the size of the corporation or what is its budget is a number of research findings in Europe and America have proven that profit making determines the nature of cultural products. Therefore the increasing emphasis on popular culture embedded in generating economic surplus. The theory of culture industry by Adorno and Horkheimer unveils this truth. (See chapter IV). If programmes of Indian media industry is analyzed the intellectuals may find that programmes by the sponsors actually reveal mass cultural products with a view to profit earning, where producers blindly borrow ideas from multinational media corporations i.e. MTV.

It has been noted that media contents of two other private channels i.e. [V] (India) and MTV (India) largely produce video music with commercial imperative.

To discuss about ZTV programmes it is noteworthy that musical programme named Sa Re Ga Ma Pa–singing Superstar 2010 basically promoting Hindi film song among the young by giving them opportunity to sing on media and by receiving monetary rewards. The strategy of the sponsors is to increase the number of consumers overnight and also make advertisement of their organizations and services. In such events public also participate to give opinion about music.

In India in case of classical music, sale of concert tickets, CDs, cassettes of classical music also indicate the colour of money. In this sense, higher music also shares with business proposition in present scenario.

Discourse on the line of cultural theories uncovers the truth that money economy and advanced technology has introduced plurality of musical culture. Moreover, like Europe and America, Indian musical culture and its relation to economy is also dialectical. In such a cultural ambience media industry acts to spread mass popular culture. Therefore, if we reassess Marxist viewpoint which emphasizes that base (economy) determines superstructure (culture) remind us the domination of economy over culture by the bourgeois in capitalist social order.

Although there are other factors of cultural productions (creativity, aims of the various classes, norms of creation etc.) still profit motivation of media investors influence the superstructure (culture) to some extent, this truth cannot be denied. In particular production of popular culture is aimed at profit making motive.

Discourse on the line of critical theories explores the fact that these theories recognize culture as a part of social totality which interprets business proposition within music is a component, objects alike any manufactured good of the marketplace. Hence, the principal of capitalism has the potential to transform art world into business world.

The underlining reason is any cultural activity need benefaction. The benefaction involves monetary assistance, whether if the work of art is creator oriented or user oriented. As stated earlier sponsoring agency pays much attention if investment would be beneficiary to business interest. In case of creator oriented art work, recording companies for release of record choose those artistes whose creations can reach to the maximum public.

7

Media and Cultural Representation

The key difference conceptualizing culture among British intellectuals initiated on the question of utility and cultural variation of highly differentiated society. Culture in this particular period became one of the central productive forces in advanced industrial societies.

The growing attention of popular music in association with music industry and screen media have been a source of temptation to many naive creators of art world now-a-days. In an era of global media cultural workers tendency towards surface style is more than depth style. The reason lies behind consumption of the mass on the one hand and on the other hand the rise of amateurs and their importance in the field of music production who balance the marketing of music trade. The new traders as well as the public, who create demand and enjoy fragmentation in creation is largely responsible for deviation of norms and imposing plurality at one's will.

The current situation has raised much concern about the norms of musical culture and institutional setting of higher music. Sign plays a dominant role in popular art form. Clothes of popular art, gesture of the artistes and song text of popular music is a representation of hedonism in the face of absolute poverty of the third world nations. Undoubtedly this very nature of popular music reveals contradictions between the agency and the society the cultural workers live.

The producers of mass culture are also involved in power game to be established like other powerful institutions e.g.

education, family and so forth. To clarify these changes a few intellectuals interpreted their cultural theory wherein conflict between high culture and popular culture is distinctly observed.

The emergence of any cultural form never depicts social harmony, rather it indicates some sort of existing social, political and economic contradictions. For instance, popular culture gained its strength at the downfall of traditional society and the dawn of capitalism and democracy.

The study of musical culture serves to provide an insight about social contradictions between individuals, groups and social structure.

Over centuries to improve personal manners through practice of higher art or becoming admirer of highbrow culture, this shared meaning of culture co-exists with other pluralistic value that reveals cultural practices of societies as culmination to transgress boundaries between high culture and popular culture. In today's context a popular song singer may feel like status he/she holds akin to court musician because masses have empowered him/her like that.

Cultural practices of contemporary Indian people simply display a sea change compared to a few decades ago since popular entertainment media industry is spreading like mushroom growth. Recently it is observed that mass culture of advanced industrial society is acting powerfully on Indian culture in particular some fraction of urban lifestyle.

Therefore, there is no reason to think that transformation on Indian soil is taking place keeping pace with the popular culture of capitalist industrial society. For India there remains a tendency to imitate whatever is happening in the developed countries. The habit of imitation in particular American and European popular culture has raised great concern to a number of intellectuals in India.

In the previous chapters Indian music is focused on theoretical line that intends in analysis subject object relationship (music and musician), its consumer, its production for the market, question of profitability in making decision to production and other capabilities (material, non-material productions of human activities) that are linked to standard of human life and social structure–investigation of these parameters provide fruitful answer of direction of social change.

A quest may arise, where lies the value in analysis of musical culture? Music as an element of culture is practiced and produced by an association of creators, receivers, benefactors and other members of culture group in the guise of economic activities. Earlier *Dhrupad* was sung in praise of the kings and nobles as a group activity during the kingdom of the Tomar and the Mughals. Later in the middle of eighteenth century *Khayal* with its improvisation came on the spotlight of court culture. Court musicians sang for the delight of the nobility like employee. In the end of nineteenth century as political unrest caused decline in usual patronage of higher music, at the same time emergence of a new business class and unfamiliar with pure classical form appreciated *Thumri-dadra* (semi-classical forms).

Music represents various aspects of human society. Various forms of musical expressions, its underlying differences in interest is interrelated to creators, audiences and other producers, has engendered several dimensions in music–namely psychological, philosophical, sociological, commercial (economic) that has been focused in previous chapters. Psychology of music generally deals with temperament, personality of musicians.

Philosophical dimension of music is linked to utopian objective that seeks salvation of soul temporarily by involving with music oneself or by the process of listening; secondly conventional philosophical connotation of music is related to aesthetic delight for both creators and listeners.

Social dimension of music conceives music as symbolic expression, because it communicates to audiences by the vehicle of sound in which feelings, emotions involve. Sociological aspects deal with interaction process between interacting parties i.e. the audience, musicians, music learners through normative standard of music. Here musical creation serves as direct object to the gratification of the need arise out of the receptors. Socio-musical phenomenon *Gharana* follows rules and regulations like other institutions.

Economic dimension involves production of music in keeping with the motif of sale. This perspective is built on the principal of power of capital that pays little attention on aesthetic logic. These three dimensions in a term is understanding sociology of music from empirical approach.

Today many Indians who can afford offerings of technological invention also share with popular culture of North America and Western Europe that is being transmitted on the part of global communication network. These media fare as well as popular musical forms have awakened new consciousness among consumers about media texts. Consciousness directed to follow style, fashion, even taste for music influenced by the westerners have enabled to foresee some segments of the society to seek new identity altering existing one. The notion of shared culture is already seen to have collapsed by the impact of western media fare.

Higher culture receives least attention since media act like a mediator to fulfil various changeable taste of the masses by production of commodity like cultural goods in particular.

This is what is happening by the expansion of commercial media industry that pays attention to popular culture demand and repays customer. Values of higher culture are thus undermined by profit making policy.

Media as a part of technology remain ready to take advantage of latest invention, for instance, popular music a few decades earlier was dependent on radio, record, cassette to be heard. Now video music captured more listeners of popular music along with the earlier facilities. Video music with its different types of texts, music, dance, style, narrative, drama fascinate audiences on account of visualize of the above mentioned texts. Music video industry is on the rise since its products appeal to the masses. Whatever novel invention takes place in developed countries India borrows blindly. The heritage of *Gharana* and its listening by political elite, aristocracy or other elite of the society is on the brink of fall since culture market displays heterogeneous mass musical culture objects. Moreover, state democracy has ensured cultural democracy on the principles of free choice. Now-a-days even elite of Indian society takes great delight in popular culture. Only a smaller portion of this class has kept themselves away from the domination of popular media fare that has the potential to evaluate cultural representation.

Looking back, model of modernization came in India in contact with British colonial rule. As a consequence, disintegration in traditional social institutions as well as traditional *Gharanas* was sharply observed. Sean Macbride says, for many people reality is obscured and distorted by messages conveyed by the media in Indian society.

Prior to independence in many aspects the notion of rationality did not work within English educated middle class. At the beginning of modernity they showed tendency to adopt western life-style, as well as interest for European literature, music, game etc.

There is no such significant change in the scenario of Indian classical music. After departure from court patronage, its infiltration in institutions, commercial broadcasting, public concert, small-scale production of cassettes, CD by recording companies, adaptive strategies for livelihood by many musicians, all these reveal classical music belonging to the mass society. Many traditional musicians perceived arbitrary expectations of the masses and reshape qualitative standard of music.

Many contemporary classical performers infuse discrete features of various *Gharanas*. As a result, presentation of music stay away from the concept of *Gharana*–it depicts basically fragmentary playing/singing style. This process of cutting, joining from various artistes, performances and signing/playing afterwards this trend of presentation music represents standardization of popular music but adopted by many artistes because public like this style is their strength. The investigation of loss of musical scholarship by this particular group is mandatory.

Moreover new invention of technology and its beneficiary use in popular music has assisted to make use of music increasingly alike other commodity of the market. For instance, contemporary remix, video music, hybrid by nature. The notion of hybrid in general is used by sociologists to refer cultural practices and values of post-colonial migrants settled other than their own country. Post-structuralist Homi Bhabha uses it to denote post-colonial migrant who can destabilize traditional identities and adopt values of the existing culture since they belong to both the East and the West. These people speak more than one language and imbibe multicultural traits because they do not belong to unified nation state.

Hybrid in musical sense I mean those mixed popular music that does not follow seriously either Indian theory of music or western musicology. These types of music are composed on shallow understanding of practical and theoretical knowledge of music.

In other words hybrid is aesthetic anarchism in the name of new music.

This type of music spoils spirit of creation and is made for money spinning formula. On the other hand effort of assimilation superficial elements of Indian music into Western popular music is evident in many cases.

Coming to the point remix music of India in matter of authorship is problematic. Its necessity lies in several issues: first Hindi film song seems to become unpopular very soon among the masses, therefore to fit it according to the taste of the buyers technological assistance receives priority. Blending, cueing, phrasing, cutting, beat juggling, scratching, all these techniques through machinery devices with pre-recorded songs, but not always blending of Hindi film songs at times mingling of Hindi, and English popular or Punjabi also receive priority. This technique is not even considered illegal by the popular media industry. Thus new technology along with the interest in profitable productivity of capitalist is playing dominant role over higher form of music by commercial triumph.

Although benefits of technology are at hand nevertheless classical music and most of its creators remain loyal to normative standard and protect itself from casual implication of technology.

The contradictory situation between higher music and pop music engender structural disintegration in the field of music.

a. Technology is capable of materialized culture leaving apart the question of subjective nature of music culture.

b. Hybrid popular music for example remix, video songs, blur distinction between music, dance, drama–a thing of the past where music was a conceived combination of Geeta, Vadya, Nrittva along with expression of body, only newness is application of mechanical devices.

c. Commercially made popular music culture and its producers are susceptible to manipulate the masses to encourage consumption of their respective cultural products. This industry may keep the youth away from higher music.

d. Compromising artistes of classical music are survivors into wider capital driven cultural life, purists are the silent sufferers.

Rapid growth of commercialized hybrid popular music, and its consumption by pleasure bound segments of the society in keeping with alternative hedonistic satisfaction of desire that most music videos manifest is not the true picture of Indian society as a whole.

Particularly role played by women in music videos represent the oldest women profession on earth, the other truths about stature of women in good profession is shadowed by pathological representation. Surprisingly the consumers of music videos belong to even educated middle class to some extent.

Apart from remix (audio, video) other videos, audio hybrid namely, Indipop, Desipop, Punjabi special, Bhangra all have influence of western sound but indigenous originally and naming appear they are in search for local identity–implicit in the meaning ambivalence. But the bottom line remains–music makers are making sense of their livelihood through music and corporate sector controlled music industry is the driving force of this dynamism in contemporary Indian society and its social life. These cultural objects are used in weddings, social parties, and pub.

Seen in pragmatic view manufacture of entertaining popular music involves many cultural workers–Deejay, music director, performer, lyricist, Bollywood star, producer, video director, dancer, choreographer, model, accountant, distributor, advertising executives. Investigation about social origin of these classes, income, taste structure, aesthetic knowledge of music makers, authenticity of these cultural products in relation to its capability to shift cultural ambience by external force is a subject matter of value judgement. Are these hybrid music are playing hegemonic role to deconstruct good taste for good music? Has technique of reproducibility (technology of recording and broadcasting) benefited classical music as it has done to popular music? So not pushing criticism one dimensionally on the interest of the entertainment media industry but from music consumer vantage point, increasing demand, its structural principle which is ascribed to it can be socio-cultural enquiry.

Summary

I have already manifested my objectives to study Indian music within the frame of cultural theory. I have argued higher music dialectically which exists in society and culture. From production and reception standpoint it seems it has reached the greatest height in modern era. In keeping with the inherent traits the bearers of popular music have already confirmed affinity with bourgeoisie interest. In this way, they have lifted their economic position from working class people. Bluntly speaking, most classical musicians who feel responsibility to aesthetic standard suffer from major setback invited by deleterious effects of industrialization of modern era. As Adorno noted some instrumentalists particularly Rossini, Berlioz, Wagner, Stravinsky embraced the verdict of demand and supply of the market, so in India, we see the similar trend. Democratic India has embraced free choice of the buyers. Expansion of the field does not necessarily indicate qualitative measures rather it indicates that artistes are the target of capitalist exploitation. More precisely capitalist hegemony is redefining the field of music at the cost of lifting moral responsibility of music world.

Master musicians directly function to form civil society by partaking in the cultural production, whose economic condition shows little difference from the class of have-nots. Moreover, belief system of higher music situate in the face of challenge as capitalists invest mostly on popular music. As a consequence heterogeneous popular music and its availability in the Indian market as well as Bangladesh speak of poor creations in the judgement of cultural elite. Despite shortcomings and contradictions in the field of traditional music, a few artistes both vocalist and instrumentalist are trying to keep pace with the customary cannons prevailing in Indian musical culture.

To understand art world, Bourdieu's concept of *habitus* might be inadequate in Indian music field since there remain other vital factors i.e. nepotism, and connection to occupy position. But his theory fully unravels the truth that musicians are living within conflicting and struggling life.

In these days, musicians are compelled to adjust with partially modern as well as traditional social system prevalent in India as well as Bangladesh. This situation voices that the field of classical music is in chain. Having considered from wider standpoint, I hesitate to put much value if the field has really achieved a lot rather it encounters dilemma. Is the process of modernity to blame or flawed democracy to blame for such phenomenon?

Social activities of Indian middle class rather explicit controversy than that of Europe. In contemporary India some middle class takes great interest from taste culture to popular culture to a greater extent. Hence, it is evident that the Indian middle class is functioning in a controversial manner.

Since the progress of the field is inter-related with many factors, higher music alone have been failing to cope with the oppositional cultural form and economic system to live with aesthetic cannons desired by the field and its bearers. What lies beneath the truth is that there prevails structural clash within the field. Emancipation of the field could be an ideology merely but struggles for fetching balance in the field is also taking place to lesser extent with the effort of a few ideologists. This situation indeed reflects that power structure also exists within the field. Class struggle and power game reveal the truth that necessity for change is inevitable in the field. Culture is no longer a single world-view rather a site of multidimensional class interest, belief system underlying economic persuasion and position making motivation in keeping with direction of the investors of the specific fields. In such realities the autonomy of art world is obviously under threat. However, the ideal creators merely experience such contradictions but average agents of popular culture are careless about ideology. Because the mediocre in cultural milieu are desperate to establish some sort of identity in association with media industry. At the same time entertainment media enterprise is free to confer status on anyone who actually does not deserve. The behavior and underlying interest of media professional give a message that the social ambience within which culture situates is a site of manipulation and pursuit of economic capital. Indeed such a situation depicts another truth that is social life is full with ambiguity, tension, competition among various agents. At the same time low taste listeners also reinforce the network of cultural work in which popular culture lives. This is the key reason why higher art enjoys status and prestige to a greater extent. Popular culture despite enormous consumers and ascribed status given by popular media giants remain in low strata in the field of cultural arena.

Bibliography

Afanasyev, V.G., Marxist Philosophy, Progress Publishers, Moscow, 1980.

Aurobindo, Sri, The Foundation of Indian Culture, Aurobindo Ashram Press, Pondicherry, 1998.

Adorno, T.W., The Philosophy of Modern Music in Anne, Michell (Trans), Sheed & Ward, London, 1973.

Adorno, T. & Horkheimer, M., Dialectic of Enlightenment, Herder and Herder, New York, 1972.

Atre, Prabha, Enlightening the Listener, Munshiram Manoharlal Publishers Pvt. Ltd., New Delhi.

Abraham, F., & Morgan, J.H., Sociological Thought: From Comte to Sorokin, Macmillan India Limited, Delhi, 1998.

Anderson, Michael, ed.,Sociology of the Family, Penguin Books Ltd., Middlesex, England, 1971.

Amarnath, Pandit, Living Idioms in Hindustani Music: A Dictionary of Terms and Terminology, Indus, An imprint of Harper Collins Publishers, India, New Delhi, 1994.

Benjamin, Walter, The Work of Art in the Age of Mechanical Reproduction in Hannah, Arendt (ed.) Illuminations, London, 1970.

Bourdieu, Pierre, The Field of Cultural Production, Essays on Art and Literature in Randal Johnson (ed.), Polity Press, Cambridge, 1993.

------------, Outline of a Theory of Practice in Richard Nice (Trans), Cambridge University Press, London, 1977.

Baran, S.J., & Davis, D.K., Mass Communication Theory, Thomson, Wadsworth, Singapore, 2002.

Bottomore, T.B., Elites and Society, Penguin Books Ltd., Middlesex, England, 1967.

Bock, P.K., Modern Cultural Anthropology: An Introduction, Alfred A. Knopf, Inc., New York, 1979.

Croce, Benedetto, Aesthetics: As Science of Expression and General Linguistic, translated by Douglas Airline, Rupa and Co., Calcutta.

Collins, Randall, Max Weber: A Skeleton Key, Sage Publications, California, 1986.

Chakroborty, M.S., Indian Musicology: Melodic Structure, Firma K.L.M. Private Limited, Calcutta, 1992.

Doshi, S.L., Modernity, Post Modernity and Sociological Theories, Rawat Publications, Jaipur, 2003.

Dube, S.E., Tradition and Development, Vikas Publishing House Pvt. Ltd., New Delhi, 1990.

Dey, S.C., The Quest for Music Divine, Ashish Publishing House, New Delhi, 1990.

Deva, B.C., An Introduction to Music, Publications Division, Ministry of Information and Broadcasting, Government of India, New Delhi, 1992.

Deva, B.C., The Music of India: A Scientific Study Munshiram Manoharlal Publishers Pvt. Ltd., New Delhi, 1981.

Deodhar, B.R., Pillars of Hindustani Music, trans., Ram Deshmukh, Popular Prakashan, Bombay, 1995.

Dastidar, N.P.G., Stepping Stone to Indian Music, J.B. Ghosh Dastidar Publisher, Calcutta, 1995.

Dasgupta, Amit, ed., Indian Horizons, Special Features, Maulana Azad Lectures, Vol. 44, No. 3, 1995, Indian Council for Cultural Relations Publications.

Danielou, Alain, Northern Indian Music: The Main Ragas, V.K. Publishing House, Delhi, 1987.

Etzioni, A. & Etzioni, E., ed., Social Change, Basic Books Inc., New York, 1964.

Eagleton, Terry, Criticism and Ideology: A Study in Marxist Philosophy, Verso, London, 1998.

Farrell, Gerry, Indian Music and the West, Clarendan Press, Oxford, 1997.

Gans, S.H., Popular Culture and High Culture, Basic Books, Inc, Publishers, New York, 1974.

Goswami, Roshmi, Meaning in Music, Indian Institute of Advanced Study, Shimla, 1995.

Goswami, B.N., Broadcasting: New Patron of Hindustani Music, Sharada Publishing House, Delhi, 1996.

Goldfarb, J.C., Civility and Subversion, Cambridge University Press, Cambridge, 1980.

Gramsci, Antonio, Selections from the Prison Notebooks, Lawrence & Wishart, London, 1972.

Gautam, M.R., Musical Heritage of India, Abhinav Publications, New Delhi, 1980.

Hamilton, J.S., Sitar Music in Calcutta: An Ethnomusicological Study, Motilal Banarsidass Publishers, Delhi, 1994.

Holroyde, Peggy, The Music of India, Praegar Publishers, New York, 1972.

Hoggart, R., The uses of literacy, Penguin, Harmondsworth, 1958.

Haralambas, M. & Heald, R.M., Sociology: Themes and Perspective, Oxford University Press, New Delhi, 1998.

Hamiltan, J.S., Sitar Music in Calcutta: An Ethnomusical Study, Motilal Banarsidass Publishers Private Limited, Delhi, 1964.

Halsey, W.D., & Friedman, E., ed., Collier's Encyclopedia, Vol. 17, Macmillan Educational Company, New York, 1982.

Joshi, O.P., ed., Sociology of Oriental Music, Illustrated Book Publishers, Jaipur, 1992.

Joshi, P.C, Culture, Communication and Social Change, Vikas Publishing House Pvt. Limited, Delhi, 1996.

Joshi, G.N., Understanding Indian Classical Music, Taraporevala Sons and Co., Private Ltd., Bombay, 1977.

Johnson, H.M., Sociology: A systematic introduction, Allied Publishers Ltd., New Delhi, 1998.

Jhangi, Rekha, Aesthetic Communication: The Indian Perspective, Munshiram Manoharlal Publishers Pvt. Ltd., New Delhi, 1985.

Kumar, K.J., Mass Communication in India, Jaico Publishing House, Mumbai, 2002.

Korsmeyor, Carolyn, ed., Aesthetics: The Big Questions, Blackwell Publishers, Oxford, 1998.

Khan, Ali Akbar, ed., The Classical Music of North India, Vol. 1 Munshiram Manoharlal Publishers Pvt. Ltd., New Delhi, 1998.

Kemp, A.E., The Musical Temperament, Oxford University Press Inc., New York, 1996.

Karnani, Chatan, Listening to Hundustani Music, Sangam Books, Bombay, 1976.

Kachroo, J.L., General Sociology, Cosmos Bookhive (P) Ltd., Delhi, 1999.

Karim, A.K. Nazmul, The Dynamics of Bangladesh Society, Nawroze Kitabistan, Dacca, 1980.

----------------, Changing Society in India, Pakistan and Bangladesh, Nawroze Kitabistan, Dacca, 1976.

Kautsky, K., Foundations of Christianity, Russell, New York, 1953.

Lakshmi, M.V., Critical Study of Sangita Makaranda of Narada, Gyan Publishing House, New Delhi, 1996.

Mutatkar, Sumati, ed., Aspects of Indian Music: A collection of essays, Sangeet Natak Akademy, New Delhi, 1987.

Mukherjee, Bimal, Indian Classical Music: Changing Profiles, West Bengal State Music Academy Publication, 1989.

Mitchell, G.D. ed., A New Dictionary of Sociology, Routledge Kegan Paul, London, 1987.

Miller, H.M., Introduction to Music: A Guide to Good Listening, Barnes and Noble Inc., New York, 1973.

Majumdar, R.C., ed., The History and Culture of the Indian People, Vol. 1, the Vedic Age, Bhartiya Vidya Bhavan, Bombay, 1965.

Mair, Lucy, An Introduction to Social Anthropology, Oxford University Press, New Delhi, 1998.

MacIver, R.M. & Page, H.C., Society, Macmillan India Limited, Madras, 1996.

Newman, W.S., Understanding Music, Harper and Row Publishers, New York and Evanston, 1961.

Neuman, Daniel M., The Life of Music in North India, Manohar Publications, New Delhi, 1980.

Nadkarni, Mohan, The great Masters: Profiles in Hindustani Classical Music, Harper Collins Publishers India, New Delhi, 1999.

Prajnananda, Swami, Historical Development of Indian Music, Ferma K.L. Mukhopadhyaya, Calcutta, 1960.

Poplcy, H.A., The Music of India, Low Price Publications, Delhi, 1990.

Pingle, B.A., History of Indian Music, Low Price Publications, Delhi, 1999.

Parmar, Sham, Folk Music and Mass Media, Communication Publications, New Delhi, 1977.

Rowell, Lewis, Music and Musical Thought in Early India, Munshiram Manoharlal Publishers Pvt. Ltd., 1998.

Rizvi, Saiyid, & Athar Abbas, A History of Sufism in India, Vol. 1, Munshiram Manoharlal Publishers Pvt. Ltd., New Delhi, 1986.

Ray, Sitansu, Studies in Music Aesthetics, Krishna Brothers Publishers, Ajmer, 1989.

Reginald and Massey, J., The Music of India, Abhinav Publications, New Delhi, 1966.

Ranade, A.D., On Musicians of Hindoostan, Promilla and Co., Publishers, New Delhi, 1984.

Roberts, Keith, A., Religion in Sociological Perspective, Dorsey Press, Chicago, 1984.

Smith, Philip, Cultural Theory: An Introduction, Blackwell Publishers, UK, 2001.

Srivastava, M.P., Social and Cultural Trends in Islamic India, Vohra Publishers and Distributors, Allahabad, 1989.

Srinivas, M.N., Caste in Modern India and other Essays, Media Promoters and Publishers Pvt. Ltd., Bombay, 1998.

Spear, Percival, A History of Delhi under the Later Mughals, Low Price Publications, Delhi, 1995.

Singh, Yogendra, Social Change in India: Crisis and Resilience, Anand Publications, New Delhi, 1996.

Sills and David L., ed., International Encyclopedia of the Social Science, Vol. 9. The Macmillan Company and the Free Press, New York, 1968.

Shringy, R.K. Trans, & Sharma, P.L., Sangita Ratnakara of Sarngdeva, Chapters II-IV, Munshiram Manoharlal Publishers Pvt. Ltd., Delhi, 1989.

Sharma, Usha, Heritage of Indian Music, Vol. II, Printwell, Jaipur, 1996.

Sharma, O.P., Indian Culture: Ancient Glory and Present Gloom, Intellectual Publishing House, New Delhi, 1993.

Sharma, Krishna, Bhakti and the Bhakti Movement: A New Perspective, Munshiram Manoharlal, Publishers Pvt. Ltd., New Delhi, 1987.

Sharma, Amal Das, Musicians of India: Past and Present, Gharanas of Hindustani Music and Genealogies, Nayar Prakash Publishers, Calcutta, 1993.

Sengupta, P. Kumar, Foundations of Indian Musicology, Abhinav Publications, New Delhi, 1991.

Sathianathan, S., Contribution of Saints and Seers to the Music of India, Vols. 1 and 2, Kanishka Publishers, Distributors, New Delhi, 1996.

Sanyal, Ritwik, Philosophy of Music, Somaiya Publications Pvt. Ltd., Bombay, 1987.

Said, E.W., Musical Elaborations, Vintage, London, 1992.

Slobada, J.A., The Musical Mind: The Cognitive Psychology of Music, Oxford University Press, 1985.

Swingewood, Alan, Cultural Theory and the Problem of Modernity, ST. Martin's Press Inc., New York, 1998.

Tumin, M.M., Social Stratification: The Forms and Functions of Inequality, Prentice Hall of India Private Limited, New Delhi, 1999.

Thapar, Romila, A History of India, Vol. 1, Penguin Books, Middlesex, England, 1987.

Tawney, R.H., Religion and the Rise of Capitalism, Penguin Books Ltd., Harmondsworth Middlesex, 1922.

Thakur, R.N., ed., Elites: Paradigm and Change in Transnational Perspective, Indian Institute of Public Administration Publication, New Delhi, 1988.

Tagore, S.M., Universal History of Music, Low Price Publications, Delhi, 1990.

Wade, B.C., Music in India: The Classical Traditions, Manohar Publishers and Distributors, New Delhi, 1997.

Wallance, Anthony, Religion: An Anthropological View, Random House, New York, 1966.

Young, V.P., Scientific Social Surveys and Research, Prentice Hall of India Private Limited, New Delhi, 1996.

Works on Bangla

Choudhary, Sucheta, Sangeet O Nandantatta, Anand Publishers Private Limited, Calcutta, 1987.

Ghosh, Pradipkumar, Sangeetshashra Samikkha, West Bengal State Music Academy, Calcutta, 1992.

Goswami, Utpala, Bharatiya Ucchanga Sangeet, Renuka Saha Publisher, Calcutta, Year 1397 (Bangla).

Maitra, Apurbashundar, Sangeet Katha, Pashchimbanga Rajja Pustak Parsad, Calcutta, 1986.

Maitra, Binota, Bharatiya Uchchanga Sangeeter Riti Bibartan, Rabindra Bharati Vishsha Vidyalaya, Calcutta, 1996.

Mukhopadhya, K., Kudrat Rangibirangi, Anand Publishers Private Limited, Calcutta, Year 1401 (Bangla).

Ray, Buddhadev, Lokasangeetikee, Firma K.L.M. Pvt. Ltd., Calcutta, 1998.

Ray, C.B., Bhartiya Sangeet Kaush, Imdadkani School of Sitar, Calcutta, Year 1391 (Bangla).

Ray, Amio, Gharawana Ki Thumri, Shambhu Roy Calcutta, 1394 (Bangla).

Index